...n his own world, John Joubert lay on the ...ver and over again, he relived the crime. ...more he saw the paperboy lying bound in ...eds, listened to his pleas for mercy, felt the ...cutting into the young flesh . . .

. . . over and over . . .

It had been perfect. Everything had gone as planned. He lay back on the bed pleasantly tired and listened to his heart hammering in his chest. This morning he had taken his fantasies a step further, and he found that he liked the feeling of power it gave him.

Now, drowsy and satisfied, the airman drifted off to sleep, his ears still ringing with the shouts:

"Please don't kill me. . . . Please . . ."

A NEED TO KILL

Mark Pettit

IVY BOOKS • NEW YORK

Ivy Books
Published by Ballantine Books
Copyright © 1990 by Mark Pettit

All rights reserved under International and Pan-American Copyright Conventions. Published in the United States by Ballantine
Books, a division of Random House, Inc., New York, and si-
multaneously in Canada by Random House of Canada Limited,
Toronto. Originally published by Media Publishing, a division
of Westport Publishers, Inc., in 1990.

Library of Congress Catalog Card Number: 88-62107

ISBN 0-8041-0785-8

Manufactured in the United States of America

First Ballantine Books Edition: April 1991

*In memory of
Danny Joe
and
Chris,
forever young*

INTRODUCTION

9:00 A.M., February 6, 1987

I had driven to Lincoln many times before but this Friday morning was different. I was more aware of the beautiful spring-like weather, the trees reaching for the crystal blue sky, and freedom in general. I was on my way to see a man who most likely will never know freedom again. Many Nebraskans hold him in as much contempt as Charlie Starkweather who, with his girlfriend, had gone on a bloody joyride which had left eleven people dead. Now, almost thirty years later, another young man had written himself into the history books.

Never before had I, as a reporter, become so wrapped up in a story, the story of a quiet, introverted young man who had unexpectedly turned into a ruthless, cold-blooded killer. A man now waiting to pay for his crimes the same way Charlie Starkweather paid for his: in Nebraska's electric chair.

For two years, I had fought for permission to interview him, keeping in touch with his attorney, waiting for this court decision then that one. Finally, afraid that he might be executed before I got a chance to talk to him, I wrote the following letter:

1-30-87
Dear John,
   For the past two and a half years I have followed ev-

1

ery step in your case. If he hasn't told you, I have also been in constant contact with your attorney, Owen Giles.

I would very much like to talk to you about the case, life on death row, and the future. Owen has been opposed to such an interview, fearing it might jeopardize your case. I now think we're past the point of damage and have decided to contact you myself. I have talked with Supreme Court Chief Justice Norm Krivosha who says anything you say now would not affect his handling of your appeal. The way the case was tried is in question—not the facts.

I feel you have quite a story to tell and must have a lot bottled up inside you. Rest assured I would be fair in giving you a chance to talk.

I'm enclosing a pre-postaged envelope and paper. At least write back. I will come to Lincoln without a crew to talk with you in person if you're interested. We'll set the ground rules for the interview. In my opinion, you have nothing to lose, but could gain a little understanding from people who wonder who John Joubert really is.

Robert Hunt (a former death row inmate) gave me his only interview—he said, "because he trusted me." You can too.
Sincerely,
Mark Pettit, Anchor/Reporter

Frankly, I did not expect a response. But five days later, the envelope came back. The station logo in the top left-hand corner had been scratched out and another return address printed neatly above it:

John J. Joubert
#35946
P.O. Box—
Lincoln, NE—

As I pulled the letter from my mail slot, I had a gut feeling that my request for an interview would be denied, but I was glad that he'd written back. I walked into an editing room, sat down, and began to read, fascinated by the level of intelligence with which the letter had been written:

02 Feb., 1987
Dear Mr. Pettit,

This is in response to your letter of 30 Jan., 1987.

Since you know that Mr. Giles has been against my participating in an interview in the past, I'm sure you can guess what his advice would be were I to ask it on this occasion. While it may be true that an interview would have no affect on my appeal, one must still consider the possibility of any new trials.

I'm not sure that I know just what story you feel I could tell, however I would not be opposed to your coming out here to present your questions if, and only if, this could be done with the understanding that I would be under no obligation to participate in an interview.

In the event that you choose not to come to Lincoln, I have two questions for you. There is no need to respond.

1) Do you see any need to air a piece which will only serve to amplify the hurt of the victims' families?

2) Do you really believe that people could watch such a piece and come away with an understanding of "who John Joubert really is?" Would they not say, rather, "It is only an act to gain our sympathy?"
Sincerely,
John J. Joubert

Two days later, I was waiting in a conference room at the Nebraska State Penitentiary for John Joubert to arrive. I'd worried the night before about how to greet him. I despised his brutal crime and was very much aware of the community's hostility toward him. Still, it's hard to talk to a person who knows you hate him. So I decided, as I'd said in my letter, neither to condemn nor condone; I would treat him like a human being. I would shake his hand.

To my surprise no guards accompanied him. Many would expect a killer to be a huge, overbearing type, but standing before me was a small, ragged-looking man in khaki prison wear, his reddish-brown hair tossed about his face. A thought ran through my mind: how small he is compared to the size of his crime. He'd put on about fifty pounds and no longer looked like the young boy who had been arrested three years before; prison had taken away the youthful softness of his face.

We now stood eye to eye. Without hesitation, I reached out and shook the hand that had stabbed two and possibly three young boys to death.

As I did in most interviews, I tried to break the ice with a few questions about his background. We discussed his childhood, the broken home, his turning to the service for direction in life. He seemed glad just to have someone to talk to, but when I began questioning him about the Eberle-Walden murders, his mood changed. His movements and speech became mechanical; he talked about what he had done in the way he might recite a poem he'd never wanted to memorize.

I listened quietly, tuning out the echoes of voices down the hall, and of phones ringing. I recalled what the guard who had walked me down the corridor had said:

"Are you nervous?"

"Just a little," I'd said.

"It's not that bad," he told me. *"Once you get past his eyes."*

Now I knew what he meant.

Joubert's eyes were a cold, gray color. Uncaring, piercing eyes. Like the eyes of a shark. There was no getting behind them, no door into his mind. And I sensed no remorse.

I hadn't expected it to turn into a full interview, but that's what it became. We talked in detail about his fantasies, which had started as a young boy. Most boys that age might have dreamed of going to Disney World; John Joubert had dreamed of killing. For two solid hours we re-lived his life, his crimes, and we discussed his future.

Before I left, I asked for a similar interview for television. I gave him several reasons why he should do it. Again, I left him a self-addressed stamped envelope.

"I'll think about it," he said.

The guard led John Joubert away, and again I was alone. I sat back in the leather, box-like chair and sorted the notebooks and papers in my briefcase. Even if he said no to the television interview I had at least satisfied some of my questions about his case.

I still could not believe that no guard had remained in the room while we talked. Occasionally, a guard would peek through the small window in the heavy wooden door, but not once were we interrupted. If I'd really wanted to hurt him there would have been nothing to stop me. I wondered what the parents of his victims would have done given the same chance.

I stuffed the rest of the papers in my briefcase and closed the lid with a click. Then I walked out of the room, pausing briefly at the guard's desk just outside.

"Thanks, guys," I said to the two men standing there. "Hopefully, I'll see you again."

"Take it easy," one of them said.

Almost two weeks later, the letter arrived. As before,

Joubert had scratched out the return address and re-placed it with his own. But this time the news was not what I had hoped:

16 Feb. 87
Dear Mark,
Please accept my apology for not answering sooner, but you left me with a lot to consider. Your reasons, particularly that of possibly preventing another from attempting murder, are most admirable (although, as I mentioned when we spoke, I don't believe that such a person would admit he had a problem), but I don't think now is the proper time for an interview.
As of yet, I have not discussed this with Owen Giles, but I shall and when we are both in agreement that an interview would do no harm to either my case or the current death penalty bill we will let you know. For whatever consolation it may afford, you can rest assured that you will be given the first—if not the only—chance of an interview when the time comes.
Thank you.
Sincerely,
John J. Joubert

Disappointed, I folded the letter, placed it back in the envelope, and walked back to my desk in the newsroom. More bad news was to come: Owen Giles, Joubert's court-appointed attorney, was leaving the case and a new Public Defender would step in.

Owen was a deeply loyal and passionate man, tireless in his battle against the death penalty. He'd spent countless hours working on the Joubert case, and although he didn't want me to talk to his client, I very much respected him. Now, I felt that my work had been in vain; if I wanted that interview, I'd have to start from scratch with another attorney.

Much to my surprise, Joubert's new attorney saw things differently than Owen Giles. Tom Garvey believed that his client should make the final decision, and that Joubert would decide by the following Sunday at noon.

Of course I was at home Sunday, and as the morning slipped away, I could feel the interview slipping away, too.

But at ten to twelve, the phone rang. I snatched up the receiver on the second ring.

"Hello."

"I have a collect call from John," the operator said, her voice sharp in my ear, "will you accept it?"

"Yes, I will."

The next words caught me off guard:

"You set up the time," John Joubert said in his low, gravelly voice, "and I'll do the interview."

"I'll call the prison first thing tomorrow."

Two years of hard work had paid off. I pushed down the button to break the connection and immediately punched in the number of my mother in Georgia. Our Sunday morning phone call had become a tradition and as usual we talked about ten minutes. I told her about John Joubert and his crimes, about what he had done to the little boys in Nebraska. She felt sorry for their families.

"I don't know what I'd have done if that had happened to one of my kids," she said. What she said next didn't surprise me: "But I also feel sorry for Joubert's mother. She may have done the best she could, and right now she's dying with him."

"I'll talk to you next Sunday," I told her. "I love you."

"I love you, too," she said.

As I hung up, I wondered for just a moment if John Joubert's mother still loved him.

I interviewed John Joubert the following Thursday. It was the first of half a dozen meetings, but the only one done on camera.

Since that day, I've traveled the country piecing together a story that has reached far beyond this small community in Nebraska. The complete case file has been put at my disposal; I've spent more hours than I can count studying its every detail and tracking down leads. The information in this book has been compiled from official records, from interviews with those directly involved, and from my own observations. I hope this book will put to rest the rumors about what happened to the victims, rumors that continue to haunt their families. Rumors about how the boys died—were they sexually molested, tortured, or worse? Rumors about whether police acted soon enough. Rumors about the man responsible.

Without the help of the victims' families, this story could never have been told. I've become close to both families. We've laughed together, cried together, and in between we've looked for answers. They've shared with me many of their deepest feelings, helped me tell the story the way it should be told, and I thank them for their courage.

We can learn a lesson from what happened; we can teach our children that there are people like John Joubert who can harm them, not only physically, but also emotionally.

Some of the names in my re-telling have been changed to protect the privacy of those involved. Other names have been changed for legal reasons. I express my sincere appreciation to the law enforcement agencies for their cooperation—The Bellevue Police Department, the F.B.I., and the Sarpy County Sheriff's

Office—and KMTV for its patience and understanding in allowing me to work on this project while at the same time continuing my duties at the station.

I must also give thanks to my friends and family for their support, for being there when I had to get some of this off my chest and for understanding why I've spent more time with my computer over the last year than I have with them. And finally, special thanks to David Kubicek for his help with the final revision of the book.

Unfortunately, what follows is a true story.

ONE

"Life is a highway with many roads branching off—don't get lost."
    (John Joubert, 1981 high school yearbook)

5:45 A.M., Sunday, September 18, 1983

In another hour, the sun would be up.

"Hey, Dan, it's time to go," Leonard Eberle called to his son from the bedroom doorway.

Thirteen-year-old Danny Joe sat up on the huge waterbed, rubbed his eyes, and yawned. The bed shook gently with the teenager's movement, but his eleven-year-old brother, Steve, didn't wake up. The boys were used to sharing the bed, and a few waves weren't about to bother either of them.

"Let's go now, Dan. Lenny's already out on his route."

Danny Joe's eyes were accustomed to the darkness, and he could make out his father's gray form clearly before him.

"O.K., I'm up," Danny Joe said, his voice almost a whisper.

Leonard Eberle quietly left the room. Danny Joe heard his footsteps becoming softer as he moved away through the house; having gotten Danny Joe and his older brother started on their paper routes, he could relax now.

Danny Joe wanted to lie down again, maybe sleep a couple more hours. He had hosted a pizza party the night before, a going-away party for his two cousins who—along with their parents—had been staying with the Eberle family. Danny Joe's uncle had lost his job in South Dakota and brought his family to Nebraska, hoping to find work. Eleven people under one roof made for a crowded house, but even at his age, Danny Joe could understand that they had troubles.

The party had lasted until eleven o'clock, much too late for a paperboy who had to be up as early as Danny Joe. Still a little groggy, he dragged himself out of bed and began to dress, slowly. He was already a veteran paperboy. He'd had his own route when the family had lived in South Dakota, and he'd now been delivering the Omaha *World Herald* for about six months. Emotionally, he was older than his age. A good portion of the twenty dollars he earned each week went toward his own school clothes and supplies. In fact, Danny Joe had stockpiled enough paper and pencils to last the rest of the school year. But he still had enough money left over to spend on his favorite passion: video games. He especially liked Pac Man, which he often played for hours at a time.

Getting up before dawn on a non-school day, however, was beginning to weigh heavily on him, and he planned to quit his route in December. He'd have plenty of money saved up by then.

The Eberles lived at 119 Valleyview Drive, a middle class neighborhood in the town of Bellevue, Nebraska.

The city of 32,000, just south of Omaha, got its name in the early nineteenth century when a French trader called it "La Belle View," which means: beautiful view. In those days, the wide, twisting Missouri River had been the main attraction for the traders, trappers, and Indians. Now the main attraction is the military. Most residents of Bellevue work at or have ties to Offutt Air Force Base, home of the Strategic Air Command (SAC). Most people think of SAC as the central nervous system of the U.S. military; others think of it as "Ground Zero."

Leonard Eberle was a short, roundish man of forty-two. In 1981, with twenty years service behind him, he had retired from the Air Force and become a mail carrier. Gray had almost completely taken over his closely-cropped beard, and it was beginning to make serious inroads into his short brown hair. Len was a soft-spoken man, strict with the children, yet easygoing.

Judy Eberle cared about her husband and children more than she cared about herself. Judy was a plain-looking, overweight woman of thirty-nine. She had short curly brown hair, green eyes, and wore glasses with brown frames. Friends described her as the perfect example of a mother hen because she always wanted to know where her children were going and when they would be back.

The Eberles lived so close to the base that if you jumped their backyard fence, you'd be on Air Force property.

On the other side of that fence, in barracks 400, room 113, the alarm clock startled Airman John Joubert from a deep sleep. He reached out, sleepily, and shut the clock off. It was awfully early for the slender twenty year old to be getting up since he hadn't worked last night, and he didn't have to work today. But he could always take a nap later. This morning there was something he just had to do.

Still half asleep, Joubert rolled out of bed. Slowly, deliberately, he slipped into his civilian clothes: blue jeans, a cotton shirt, tennis shoes. After dressing, he picked up the long, thin filet knife from the table and slipped it into the sheath on his belt. Then he walked out into the warm, dark morning.

Danny Joe Eberle was a five-foot-two-inch, 100-pound bundle of energy and as scrappy as they come. Brownish-blonde hair and a square-jaw set off by deep crystal blue eyes made his face glow with health. The teenager was a hard worker and knew his customers counted on him; they expected their papers by breakfast so they could scan the front page news. He usually finished delivering to the seventy houses on his route by eight o'clock.

The house was quiet, but Danny Joe could hear soft voices in the driveway. He moved toward the front door and stepped outside.

"We can't thank you and Len enough," he heard Aunt Joanne say as she embraced his mother in the early morning darkness.

"We'll miss you," Judy said.

It was both a happy and a sad morning at the Eberle home. Jo Ann Schatz and her family were heading home so Tom could start his new job at the coal plant in South Dakota. With five children of her own, Judy was happy to be getting her house back, but she would very much miss her twin sister.

"Well, look who's finally out of bed," Uncle Tom announced as Danny Joe came down the front steps and joined the others near the U-Haul truck in the driveway. "Where are your shoes, boy? Can't do any girl chasing without shoes!"

Danny Joe glanced down sheepishly at his bare feet.

"Ain't no girls to chase at this time of the morning," he said with a laugh, drawing laughter from the rest of the family as well.

He enjoyed the razzing from his uncle and was always quick with the comebacks.

"Now, Danny," Judy Eberle said, "I want you to give Auntie Jo Ann and Uncle Tom a big hug before they leave."

"Oh Mom. . . ." the boy sighed, giving his mother one of those I'M TOO BIG FOR THAT looks.

Judy shot her son one of those DO WHAT I SAY looks.

Without another word, Danny Joe embraced his aunt, then his uncle, and told them how much he'd miss them and that he would surely come for a visit soon.

"I love you, too," he finished.

Then it was time for business. With a smile and a wave, the boy was off on his paper route.

As she watched her son peddle his bicycle up the sidewalk, Judy Eberle felt a sudden uneasiness. Without realizing it, she stepped away from the others, tuned out the talk, the good-byes. Danny Joe moved farther and farther up the hill, farther into the darkness. Some deep buried instinct urged her to call out to him, to plead with him to return to the family circle where he was safe, where people loved him. But she shrugged off this mother's intuition.

"Don't be silly, Judy," she told herself. "Don't be silly."

TWO

"In my mind these were simply recreational murders. Some people go out and play a game of racquetball, he [Joubert] goes out and kills a little kid."

(Prosecutor Mike Wellman)

Outside the Kwik Shop John Joubert took the last swig of his Mountain Dew, his favorite drink, and tossed the empty bottle with a clunk into a nearby trash can. Although the airman didn't see it, ten feet to his right, securely fastened to a lightpole by metal bands, was a "Neighborhood Watch" sign, warning would-be criminals that people in the neighborhood were looking out for one another.

Across the street in the Dairy Queen parking lot, a boy was down on his hands and knees, efficiently rolling newspapers and slipping rubber bands around them. Most of the papers had already been banded.

When the boy finished, he climbed onto his bike and pedaled across the street to begin his route. Joubert got into his tan 1979 Nova and turned the key in the ignition. The engine rumbled to life. John Joubert pulled out of the convenience store parking lot and followed the boy.

To avoid looking suspicious, the airman drove past the paperboy and pulled into a gravel parking lot behind the home of a local dentist. Quickly, like a surgeon before an operation, he slipped on a pair of clear plastic gloves that he'd gotten at the base hospital. Then he got out, closed the door, and started up the walk toward the boy. He did not hurry.

Danny Joe Eberle looked up at the approaching stranger. "Hello," he said.

"Hello," the stranger mumbled, brushing past.

The curt greeting surprised the teenager, but his good nature would not let him dwell on it. He reached into his bag for one of the papers and tossed it at a front porch where it landed with a quiet slap.

Danny Joe did not notice that the man had stopped to watch him. He watched the boy deliver the first paper, then the second, then the third. . . .

As Danny Joe mounted his bike to move on to the fourth house, a hand grasped his shoulder. He jumped and looked up into the face of the man he'd passed only a few minutes ago.

Danny Joe tried to think of something to say, but all that came to mind was: "Hello."

At that point, the boy didn't really feel afraid, but it was odd. What did the man want?

Joubert clamped a hand over Danny Joe's mouth.

Slowly, he drew the thin blade from its sheath with the whispering sound of metal against leather. He held the knife up so the boy could see. Danny Joe's eyes widened. Now he was afraid.

"Don't make any sounds," Joubert said. "Come with me."

The boy dropped his bike and bundle of papers against the stone gray Cyclone fence around the dentist's home. Joubert walked Danny Joe across the parking lot, their footsteps crunching softly on the gravel. Somewhere, there was the dull rumble of traffic as the city began waking up.

"Here," Joubert said, tugging on Danny Joe's head. "Stop."

The airman looked around, but in this area there was as yet very little traffic.

"Lie down. On your stomach."

Danny Joe obeyed, trembling inside. He tried to speak, but he was too terrified.

"Put your hands behind your back."

Danny Joe pulled his hands up behind him. He heard the car door open, heard something being dragged across the floor. He felt his hands being bound together, then his feet. Roughly, he was rolled over and found himself staring into the face of his kidnapper.

Joubert's breathing was heavy, ragged. He dug in his pocket for a roll of wide surgical tape, tore off a strip, and pressed it firmly over the boy's mouth.

Danny Joe didn't make a sound; he lay very still, as if he were dead.

John Joubert stood up and opened the trunk of his car. After checking for traffic and seeing none, he picked up the boy and placed him in the trunk. Then he pushed down the lid with a solid thump. Although he didn't realize it at the time, the airman had pulled his car into the parking lot of the Pilgrim Lutheran Church. Across the street was the Bellevue Church of Christ. In a few hours, both churches would be full of people praying for the less fortunate. Next Sunday, they would be praying for Danny Joe Eberle.

It was a bumpy four and a half mile drive to Base Lake Road and the open field where John Joubert would complete his business. Although his hands were sweating, he didn't dare take off the gloves. Finally he reached his destination and pulled off to the side of the gravel road, just past a sign that read "Dead End." It would be just like the stories in those detective magazines, Joubert thought as he got out of the car. Himself in total control; his victim helpless.

Joubert opened the trunk and lifted Danny Joe in his

arms and carried him to a grassy ditch five feet away. The hum of the nearby Allied Chemical plant masked the more delicate morning sounds. The plant's lights gave an eerie orangish glow to the sky. Had it been Monday, the shift soon would be changing, and a stream of workers would be flowing in and out of the plant. But it was Sunday, and John Joubert and the boy were alone.

Joubert closed the lid, and walked unhurriedly back to where his victim lay. Danny Joe's wrists and ankles hurt, and the tape was pulling at his skin. The freshness of the morning was mingled with the musty smell of the grass. His heart was beating very fast as the man approached him again.

Joubert knelt down, loosened the rope from the boy's hands and yanked it off.

''Take off your shirt.''

Danny Joe did as he was told. The man then untied the boy's feet and tugged off his pants, but left him wearing his underpants. Joubert was breathing heavily again as he re-tied Danny Joe's hands; he was becoming very excited. By this time, the surgical tape had slipped just enough for Danny Joe to speak, but he remained silent, his eyes riveted on the man's face.

Then Joubert drew the knife, slowly, savoring the moment; he enjoyed the sense of power it gave him. The morning light made the blade gleam dully. Sensing danger, the paperboy squirmed, but his movements were too feeble to do any good.

''Please don't kill me,'' he pleaded.

John Joubert plunged the knife into the boy's back. The teenager gasped at the red-hot streamer of pain that lanced through his body.

''Please. . . . '' he begged. ''Just take me to the hospital. I won't tell!''

It's too late, John Joubert thought. . . . Things had gone too far; he couldn't stop now.

Four more times, he plunged the knife into the boy's back. Then four times in the chest. To make sure that the boy was dead he slashed the back of his neck.

Still not satisfied, Joubert began to bite the boy's body. Once on the upper backside of his left leg, twice on the upper left shoulder. Then Joubert picked up the knife again; where he had bitten the boy's leg, he carved a star-like design.

His fantasy now completed, John Joubert stood up and looked at what he had done. In one way, he felt proud; in another way, ashamed. He had, however, very much enjoyed the experience.

He looked at his hands, sticky with drying blood. Instantly, he wiped them on the boy's clothing. Then he wiped the knife, taking pains to get as much of the blood off as he could, and slid it into its sheath. The pants and shirt he flung into the field of milo running along the ditch, then dragged the boy's body farther into the high weeds so that it couldn't be easily spotted from the road.

Now the sun hung low above the horizon, and suddenly Joubert was afraid. He'd been so wrapped up in his task that he hadn't even noticed how light it was getting. He glanced quickly, nervously around. Still, he was alone, he and the boy.

Hurriedly, Joubert climbed into his car. The engine seemed unnaturally loud in the morning stillness. If it had been a little lighter, he might have seen the rusty sign nailed to a telephone pole just a few yards away: "No Hunting Or Trapping Under Penalty Of Law."

As John Joubert put his car in gear, he was suddenly aware of the hunger gnawing at his insides. He ripped off the plastic gloves and tossed them into the passenger seat. Then he headed for town and the local McDonald's where he had a hearty breakfast.

THREE

"It's easy to kill little kids. No matter how many law enforcement officers you have, it's easy to kill little kids. We wanted to stop him before he killed again."
(Sheriff Pat Thomas)

"So much for a little sleep," Judy told her husband as she slipped back into bed. "Danny must be running behind on his route."

It wasn't even 7:00 A.M., but the phone was already ringing back at the Eberle house. Two calls within minutes of each other from people who had not yet received their morning papers. Nothing was wrong, she assured herself. It had happened before. The drop-off truck was probably just late.

Maria Eberle took the next call. Maria was a petite girl with shoulder-length wavy blonde hair and a dimple in her left cheek. When she smiled, her dark brown eyes seemed to sparkle.

Danny Joe's supervisor was on the line.

"Let me get my dad," Maria said.

Len Eberle went to the kitchen and picked up the extension. People were calling in, the supervisor explained, complaining about not getting their papers.

"I've already looked for him myself. I can't find him anywhere along his route."

"I'll meet you at 23rd and Mission," Len said and hung up.

Feeling a little uneasy, he returned to the bedroom.

"That was Danny Joe's boss," he said from the doorway. "They can't find him anywhere."

Immediately, Judy got up and began to dress. Len began to dress, too. They put on the first pieces of clothing they could find and were soon out the door to look for their son.

It wasn't like Danny Joe to miss a customer's house, let alone desert his route.

Something was terribly wrong.

Three houses into Danny Joe's route, they found his bike, leaning against the fence at the dentist's home. A few feet away lay his bag of papers, a rock placed upon them so they wouldn't scatter in the wind.

Judy wished that she had heeded her feeling of uneasiness that morning, that she had not let her son go out.

"Let's go to the police station," Len Eberle said as they got back into the car.

He tried to keep his voice even, tried not to let her guess what he was thinking; she might lose control if she guessed. Building inside him was the feeling that the worst thing that could have happened had happened.

No. He wouldn't accept that. He just couldn't accept it.

But neither could he force the thought from his mind.

At the Bellevue police station, things were quiet. Things were usually quiet on a Sunday morning. The dispatcher smiled warmly at the Eberles as they approached the counter.

"Can I help you folks?" she said.

"Our son's missing from his paper route," Len said.

The woman saw the desperation in his eyes and immediately radioed for help. The Eberles stood silently until the dispatcher turned back to them.

"An officer's on the way," she said. "Would you like some coffee?"

Len and Judy shook their heads.

Within a few minutes, the officer was back at the station and had the Eberles filling out forms.

"We'll be out there looking for him," the officer told them. "Why don't you go home in case he calls."

Soon after the Eberles returned home, the phone rang. Judy snatched up the receiver.

"Hello!"

"Mrs. Eberle?" A woman's voice. Judy's chest felt hollow with disappointment. "Sorry to bother you, Mrs. Eberle, but I think Danny Joe missed our house this morning."

"Ma'am," Judy said, "Danny Joe's missing from his route, and we're trying to find him right now."

The woman was sympathetic and did not press further.

But as soon as Judy hung up, the phone rang again. This time, the caller was not so understanding.

"Just like damn kids these days," he said. "He's probably run off or something."

"Totally irresponsible," Judy heard him mutter. Then a violent click in her ear followed by a dial tone.

After three more calls like that one, Leonard Eberle refused to answer the phone. But Judy had to answer. One of them might be Danny Joe, phoning from a friend's house to tell them that he was all right.

Soon officers from the Bellevue Police Department arrived, and they asked a lot of questions. Judy could not understand what some of their questions had to do with Danny Joe's disappearance. Her son was missing, and here the police were asking idiotic questions. Why didn't they go out and find him?

"What was Danny's homelife like?"

"Were there any problems?"

"Could he have run away?"

"Did he say anything that might have given a clue?"

It didn't take long for the officers to be convinced that Danny Joe was not a runaway; this boy was not the kind to leave home without telling his parents where he was headed. Nor was he likely to go away with people he didn't know; only two weeks before, he had scored 86 out of 100 on a test about not going with strangers.

When fifteen-year-old Lenny returned from his route, his father explained that Danny Joe was missing.

"Why don't you go finish Danny's route," Leonard Eberle said.

"How can you worry about the paper route!" Maria demanded. Then she turned on her mother. "We should all be out looking for him!"

Neither parent spoke. Maria looked at her father, then at her mother.

"Don't you care about him?" she asked, her cheeks wet with tears.

"Of course we care about him," Judy said. "But honey, we don't even know where to start. The police are looking for him, and we have to be here in case he calls."

That did not pacify Maria, who had already formed a search party of friends. She stormed to the door and yanked it open.

"I'll find him then!" she yelled, slamming the door behind her.

Back in his own world, John Joubert lay naked on the bed. Over and over again, he relived the crime. Once more he saw the mostly-undressed paperboy lying bound in the weeds, listened to his pleas for mercy, felt the knife cutting into the young flesh . . .

. . . over and over. . . .

* * *

It had been perfect. Everything had gone as planned. Once again, the feeling of power was arousing him. Slowly, he began to masturbate. He could still hear the paperboy begging for his life.

"Please don't kill me. . . . Please don't kill me. . . . Please. . . ."

The words echoed inside Joubert's head, like shouts in a cave.

In only a few minutes, he brought himself to a violent climax, then, breathing heavily, he lay back on the bed pleasantly tired and listened to his heart hammering in his chest. Masturbating had become a ritual. Sometimes he did it three times a day, always after glancing through his stack of true crime magazines. But this morning, he had taken his fantasies a step further, and he found that he liked the feeling of power it gave him.

Now, drowsy and satisfied, the airman drifted off to sleep, his ears still ringing with the shouts:

"Please don't kill me. . . . Please. . . ."

FOUR

*"There's still fear . . . this long after. I see peo-
ple on the street today who say they're still fearful, their children are fearful."*
(Sheriff Pat Thomas)

*Shoulder pads colliding, a shout from the crowd, now
and then the high-pitched shriek of the referee's whistle.*

John Evans stood on the sidelines at Kingswood Park
in west Omaha, enjoying the warm day and watching
his little league football team in action. He was proud
of his boys. The "Packers" had won all of their games
this season and appeared well on the way to another
victory.

A short, stout man of forty-three, Evans was second
in command of the Omaha F.B.I. office. Before that,
Evans had been a teacher in his home town of Lock-
land, Ohio, where he'd also coached high school football. In 1965, by a stroke of fate, his career had taken
a sudden turn. He and his wife had chaperoned a senior
class trip to Washington, D.C., and while waiting for a
tour to begin, Evans had wondered aloud if the F.B.I.
still was accepting only lawyers and accountants as
agents. The tour guide overheard his question.

"With your master's degrees," the tour guide said,
"you might qualify."

This intrigued Evans. That same year he applied and
was accepted into the Federal Bureau of Investigation.

As an agent, he had worked on some interesting cases, but he was most proud of one accomplishment that had nothing to do with law enforcement: he'd coached two young men who'd gone on to play in the N.F.L. Football was still his passion, and he was glad that his eleven-year-old son, Matt, had inherited some of that enthusiasm.

Suddenly, the shrieking of his electronic pager broke the morning excitement. Evans's instinctive reaction was annoyance, then he felt uneasy. On a Sunday morning, it could only mean bad news; few bank robbers or extortionists worked weekends.

Many a night, John Evans had lain awake worrying that a recent crime in Iowa might be repeated. A young paperboy named Johnny Gosch had apparently been kidnapped while delivering the Sunday *Des Moines Register*. The case, almost a year old, had never been solved. The boy's parents had accused police and the F.B.I of not following up on leads.

My God, it's happened again, John Evans thought, as he turned off the pager.

"I've got to go make a call," he told one of his assistant coaches.

A friend lived a block and a half down the street, and John Evans ran all the way. Quickly, he punched the office number and waited.

"What do you want?" he asked, panting, his mouth full of an irony taste.

"Call Chief Robinson in Bellevue," the agent said.

Evans hung up and punched the Bellevue Police Department's number. Soon Chief Warren Robinson came on the line.

"John, we've got a boy missing over here . . . he's a news boy."

Des Moines again. Johnny Gosch. Missing.

While Evans listened patiently, Chief Robinson explained the circumstances of the disappearance. The boy could have gone off to be by himself, he knew. He could be a runaway. He could be missing for any number of reasons. John Evans hoped to God that it wasn't foul play, not another *Johnny Gosch*.

But they had to treat it as if it were a kidnapping.

"I'll send an agent right over, Robbie," Evans said.

That morning several agents in the F.B.I.'s Omaha office had taken part in the Corporate Cup Run, a local competition made up of team members from the same company. The year before the F.B.I. team had taken first place, but this year it was different; the Bureau had come in second. Team captain Chuck Kempf was not at all happy with the situation, but he was looking forward to the get-together at a friend's cabin on Hansen Lake.

Small and wiry, Kempf at forty-one was in tremendous shape and stayed that way by running every day. Earlier that year he had become the physical fitness advisor at the office.

Kempf got home from his run just before noon and had one foot in the shower when the phone rang.

. . . A paper boy was missing. He was needed. His boss would meet him. . . .

Chuck Kempf sighed as he dropped the receiver into its cradle.

So much for the party, he thought.

John Evans had phoned his office to ask for a complete copy of the Gosch file; it was waiting for him when he arrived at the Bellevue Police Station. He sat down at a desk to compare the two cases. The F.B.I. hadn't entered the Gosch case until long after the boy had disappeared. Now, looking at the two together, Evans shivered at their similarity:

Two young boys.

Both delivering papers.
Both gone without a trace.
No witnesses:

Evans still believed that Danny Joe Eberle could be off somewhere by himself, upset over his favorite uncle leaving town.

I wonder if the kid could have stowed away in the U-Haul? Evans thought.

He put out an all points bulletin for the Schatz family, who by this time would be well on their way to South Dakota. But the police didn't know that the Schatzes had decided to take the scenic route, staying off the main roads, and the truck would not be spotted for several hours.

John Evans was still at Bellevue Police Headquarters when the call came at 12:19 A.M. the next morning. He rubbed his eyes wearily and lifted the receiver.

"John, Danny Joe's not with them," said the agent on the line.

It was if Evans's heart had turned to stone. Until now he hadn't realized how much he had counted on the boy being with that truck.

Dark clouds were now rolling into the metro area, and the weathermen were predicting rain and colder weather. Evans knew that Danny Joe was barefooted. If he were hiding somewhere in Fontenelle Forest, he could become sick from exposure. The case was looking more and more like a kidnapping.

Members of the media were more than helpful to the distraught parents. All three television stations broadcast Danny Joe's description and picture on the evening news. Radio stations aired the story every hour. And Monday morning, the *World Herald* carried a front page photo of the young man who had been so punctual in delivering the paper.

Evans decided it was time to bring Pat Thomas into

the case. As the Sarpy County Sheriff, he was the top lawman in the area. If a full scale investigation were to develop, he would have to be part of it.

Physically, Thomas was everything you'd expect a sheriff to be: 6'4'', 250 pounds, his burly appearance diffused by his quiet, business-like demeanor. His gray-streaked brown hair, combed straight back and barely touching his oversized ears, could pass for a military cut. His blue eyes and dimple in his chin made him resemble a boy who had never lost all of his baby fat. Thomas had grown up on a farm, and a college education and stint in the military had failed to citify him. He was a self-proclaimed "fried potatoes" kind of guy.

For six and a half years he had taught school in Bellevue, and his concern for children had led him into law enforcement; he'd left teaching after being offered the position of Sarpy County Youth Programs Coordinator—which was, as Thomas said, a fancy name for probation officer. In his new job, Thomas saw beaten and battered children, little girls who'd been victims of incest, everything. He saw enough to make him sick for the rest of his life.

At the time, Thomas had had no higher ambitions for law enforcement. At least not until the then-sheriff was indicted on gambling charges by a federal grand jury and had to leave office. Suddenly, Thomas found himself the leading candidate for the job. On September 5th, 1973, he was appointed, and he'd been sheriff ever since.

Pat Thomas did not get along with Police Chief Warren Robinson. Robinson believed that Thomas was out to take over the county, and Thomas did favor consolidation as a way to save taxpayer dollars. But the hard fact was: Thomas didn't respect Robinson as a lawman. They were from different schools of thought. Robinson knew how the political game worked, but Thomas didn't think

of law enforcement as a game. It was work, and sometimes very unpleasant work involving real people and
real emotions. Law enforcement to Thomas was not
moving little ivory figures around a chess board. But
despite their differences, Robinson didn't object to
Thomas entering the investigation. The two men could
put their jobs ahead of their personal problems.

The investigators quickly assembled a task force. It
was comprised of officers from the Bellevue Police Department, the Sarpy County Sheriff's Department, and
the F.B.I. Twenty-three year veteran Captain Don Carlson led the agents from the Bellevue P.D., Lt. Jim Sanderson was lead investigator for the Sheriff's office, and
Evans for the F.B.I. He chose Agent Chuck Kempf to
be his right-hand man.

Sanderson, a rangy, sandy-haired man of thirty-two,
was chosen to lead the task force. His boyish face was
dusted with freckles, and his eyes seemed always to be
filled with wonder. If you didn't know better, you'd
have sworn he was Opie Taylor grown up. His law enforcement career had begun in 1970 when he was hired
as a $350 a month dispatcher by the Bellevue Police
Department while still attending the University of Nebraska in Omaha.

Sanderson's colleagues considered him a first-rate
cop, the logical one to be in charge. But Sanderson was
not so sure. To be suddenly thrust into the limelight, to
be responsible for sending 150 officers out to check
every possible lead, was the greatest challenge of his
career.

Because of its central location, the Bellevue police
station became the command center.

"You all know the facts of the case," Jim Sanderson
told his officers Monday morning. "We have to talk to
every person who saw the boy in the last month. Somebody has to know something."

The hotline began ringing as soon as it was established. Hundreds of calls poured into the command center. Many came from people who thought they'd seen Danny Joe. Other calls came from "psychics" who offered to help police find the missing boy.

Two days passed, and still no sign of Danny Joe. The officers could feel the pressure, like a pall hanging over the station. Lieutenant Sanderson was a new father himself. He and his wife, Terrilyn, had a one-month-old daughter, so he could understand what the Eberle family was going through. He dreaded telling them what they had to know: it was time to stop looking for the boy and start looking for his body.

But John Evans still clung to the shred of hope that Danny Joe was all right, that he'd gone off by himself to be alone. He might be ill, but he would be found alive.

The next logical step was an organized search, and if a search were to be done, Evans wanted it done right. He called in an expert from Sioux City.

"Here's a map of the county," he told the man. "Where do we start?"

Sanderson put out a call for additional manpower, and lawmen from several neighboring counties headed for Bellevue.

John Kolterman, Chief of Police from the small town of Wahoo, was one of them. The Chief didn't know exactly what he could do in Bellevue; the operation was being kept so secret. And had it not been for the morning paper, he might have found himself grossly overdressed. The headline stretched across page one of the Omaha *World Herald*:

130 OFFICIALS TO SEARCH 9-1/2 SQUARE MILES TODAY FOR DANNY JOE EBERLE

Beneath these words was a story explaining that this would be a search for his body.

Chief Kolterman exchanged his coat and tie for blue jeans and oxfords, clothing much more suitable for the fields through which he would soon be tramping. A baseball cap atop his 6'3" frame and his police jacket for protection against the morning chill completed his dress.

The last time Kolterman had worked a murder case was back in March of 1969; he'd been a rookie on the Wahoo police force.

Sixteen-year-old Mary Kay Heese had disappeared one day on her way home from school. A search of the town had turned up no clues. Then, at midnight, a farmer working his fields came across school books in the middle of a dirt road. In the ditch a few feet away, he found Mary Kay's body. She had been stabbed several times. The murder had shocked the small community; it had never been solved. Since that day long ago, the word "murder" rarely found its way into the local paper—unless it was a story out of Omaha.

Chief Kolterman felt an emotional tie to the Eberle family. He could empathize with them. Only two months before, his own son had died in a car crash; Jim was only sixteen years old.

Chief Kolterman, Saunders County Sheriff Ron Proskochill, and one of his deputies made the forty-five minute drive to Bellevue together. As they wound through the countryside, Chief Kolterman began to think out loud.

"There's simply no way we're going to find that boy," he said. "Look at all those hills."

The other two men looked, and they shook their heads.

"He could be buried anywhere," the Chief went on, "or floating in the river for all we know."

The sheriff concurred.

"There's no way in hell we're going to find him," Chief Kolterman repeated.

They divided the county into sections. Sanderson, Evans, and Carlson decided to start at the river and work west. The area around Base Lake Road would be as good a place as any to begin their search.

"First of all," Sanderson told the officers gathered in the recreation pavilion near the lake, "let me thank you all for coming to help us in this search. As you know, we're looking for a thirteen-year-old boy who's been missing for three days now. Each of you have been assigned to a team and given an area to cover. I'd like those of you that don't know him to meet Chuck Kempf from the F.B.I. He'll say a word then divide you into teams."

"There are seven teams," Kempf said, "and each group has a team leader. That person will keep everything organized and will make sure that the search is thorough. Should you come across something, please don't disturb the evidence. Pick up the radio and call in. The code word is 'package.' If you find something, that's what you should call it."

Everyone knew what that something was.

The orientation completed, the searchers broke up into teams of four. Standing an arm's length apart, they spread out across the grassy field. Unknown to them, John Joubert was working on radar systems only a few hundred yards away.

The men from Wahoo had gotten a late start, and the search was already in progress when they arrived. John Kolterman, Sheriff Proskochill, and the deputy were quickly teamed with an F.B.I. agent and an officer from the local police department. The group was assigned to area seven, a gravel path just off Base Lake Road. The F.B.I. agent drove the truck while the other team mem-

bers fanned out in the field. Chief Kolterman clumped
through the ditch along the edge of the road.

The search lasted twenty minutes.

"Here it is!" the Chief shouted, sounding as if he
were the winner of some morbid treasure hunt. "I found
it! I found a body."

Team leader Mike Hally from the F.B.I. picked up
his walkie talkie from the seat of the truck.

"Team leader seven to command post. . . ."

"Go ahead, seven," came Chuck Kempf's voice.

"We found the package."

Kempf was caught off guard; he hadn't expected anything so soon. But he didn't waste time mulling it over.

Soon police radios were crackling with the news.
Within a few minutes, more than a dozen lawmen were
hovering over the tiny body. They worked in a hushed
business-like fashion. Some took measurements of how
far the body was from the road. Another searcher ran
a metal detector over the grass near the body and
through the edge of the milo field, hoping to find the
murder weapon or at least some clue that might help
them.

Kempf looked down at the boy, clad only in his underwear, his small hands clutched near his back. His
wounds seemed to stand out in relief. It was a sight that
would change Chuck Kempf forever. Suddenly, he realized that something was missing from his life. He'd
been concerned only about himself for so long; maybe
it was time to settle down, time to start a family of his
own. The death of a little boy he had never known had
so shaken Kempf that the thought of it would bring tears
to his eyes for many years to come.

Sheriff Pat Thomas was at the command center when
word came that the search had ended. He went immediately to the open field just off Base Lake Road to find
out first hand what had happened.

The boy lay face down in the weeds, his hands and feet still bound with rope.

"My God," Thomas said to Lieutenant Jim Sanderson. "Some bastard thinks he's a butcher."

Sanderson nodded. He shivered, not entirely from the icy wind penetrating his summer sport coat. The day the paperboy had disappeared, it had been sunny and the high had been seventy-seven degrees. Now, three days later, the mercury was hovering near freezing. Like the Eberle case, the weather had taken a sudden turn for the worse.

Sheriff Thomas had seen a lot during his twenty-plus years in law enforcement, but nothing like this, nothing like what he would see over the next four months. Later, he would call it the most pressure he'd ever been under—not at all what the doctor recommended for a man who had just the year before had triple bypass heart surgery.

After he'd seen the body, John Evans went to the Bellevue police station to call his boss, Herb Hawkins. The two men had been friends for years. No federal law had been broken, and the F.B.I. could pull out at any point.

"What do you want to do, John," Hawkins asked. "You tell me."

"We have no choice, Herb. We've got to stay with it."

Hawkins did not question Evan's judgement, and his next words were not spoken in anger:

"Don't leave Bellevue until you solve it."

Later that night while the cameras clicked and flashed, Sheriff Thomas tried to answer the reporters' questions. He knew that whoever had killed Danny Joe Eberle was probably watching.

"We don't know if the victim was sexually assaulted,'' he told a reporter from one of the television stations, ''and no, we haven't found a murder weapon.''

There were, however, certain things he couldn't tell the media—that the victim's body had been bitten, for instance, and not by an animal. Nor could he tell them what he knew deep in his gut: they had to find the murderer fast or he would almost certainly kill again.

On October 5th, 1983, the following letter appeared in the Bellevue *Leader*:

> *Where is it safe for a child to play?*
> *Does it matter whether night or day?*
> *In a park, school ground or on your front lawn.*
> *Look away for a moment, a child is gone.*
>
> *What could possibly possess someone to be so cruel? What will the world come to, when will it end?*
>
> *Where does the main problem lie? Children are much more trusting today than years ago. Their parents tell them, "Don't talk to strangers." But, what about the child that does not get the attention they need at home? The child that goes to school, gets good grades, comes and goes as he or she pleases, and is never really noticed by their family. I feel that parents should get closer to their children. Talk to them and let them know you care.*
>
> *You can ask yourself another question. What or who is a stranger? What about the stranger with a kind face and warm smile? The eyes and ears of children seem to be taken in by someone who shows them kindness, not knowing the deceit behind the smile. It could be someone you have known for years, seeing only what they appear to be, when the stranger lurks within. Can no one be trusted?*
>
> *Children must be made aware! There are various assault and rape awareness classes available to adults. But what about a Child Awareness Class?*

Children must be made aware that it could happen to them and it doesn't have to be a stranger.

To the Eberle family the nightmare is over, the pain just beginning. My prayers are with them as well as all the missing children and their families. But what will happen to the madman who committed such a violent crime? Will he plead insanity or get off on a lesser charge? When will the court systems become more strict with the sentences of murderers, rapists etc.? How many more children must disappear before the courts stop protecting the offenders? There can not be any justification, consolation or forgiveness for such a crime!

Children are our tomorrow. They hold the key to the future. We must take the time to understand them. They must be protected.

Another search ended.

A body found.

Guard well the children, there are strangers around. (Dana Jean Graziano, SRA, U.S. Air Force, Offut AFB)

A few years later, police cars in Bellevue would carry the credo "Let None Live In Fear" emblazoned on the front doors. But over the next several weeks, almost everyone in town would live in fear, fear that a son, a daughter, a brother or sister could be next.

FIVE

"I remember when we would wrestle; he was so strong there were times I thought he had the best of me. I will go to my grave wondering why Danny Joe didn't fight back."

(Len Eberle)

Len Eberle was well into his route when his supervisor's blue car pulled up behind his mail truck, and he was suddenly afraid. Judy had pleaded with him not to go to work that morning. He wished now that he had heeded her.

Len's boss and another man stepped out of the car, and Len slowly approached them.

"Did they find him?" he asked.

"We don't know, Len," his boss said. "They just told us to bring you home."

Len and his supervisor got into the car and drove away; the other man stayed to finish Len's route.

"Come on, Ron," Len said, "didn't they tell you anything?"

No answer.

"Ron, tell me something."

The silence made it worse. Len Eberle had an aching feeling in his chest that he would never see his son alive again. When he walked through his front door and saw the priest, his suspicions were confirmed. Judy got up slowly from the sofa and hugged her husband.

"It's over," she whispered. "They found him."

"Len, we're not sure it's Danny Joe," Sheriff Thomas said, trying to extend one last thread of hope.

That irritated Len Eberle.

"Don't hold anything back," he said, frowning.

"We'll need you to come down to the morgue," Thomas said. "For identification."

It was a ten minute drive to the Douglas County Hospital in downtown Omaha where the boy would be autopsied. Sheriff Thomas drove while Len sat quietly, staring out the window at the seemingly endless procession of streetcorners, storefronts, and traffic lights. At first, Len had felt anger, but the anger had quickly turned to rage, then to hate.

How could anyone do this to a child?

He was torn between wanting to know everything that had happened to his son and wanting to know nothing. He preferred to remember Danny as he had been. Len smiled, recalling his son's positive outlook on life, his cheerful personality, his happy smile. A memory came to him.

Len and Danny had been washing dishes after supper one night.

"I want to build a go-cart, Dad," Danny Joe had said proudly. "But I don't know what size motor to use."

The announcement hadn't surprised Len. Danny Joe was always coming up with ideas for projects, and Len had learned from experience that the boy could do almost anything he set his mind to.

"Don't worry, son," he said. "We'll find the right motor."

"Great! It won't take me long to save up the money."

The simple times together were what Len Eberle cherished most. How he wished that his son could have lived to build that go-cart.

"Wait here," Sheriff Thomas whispered. "I'll be back in a few minutes," he said as the two men walked into the morgue.

Len nodded and sat down on a chair against the wall. Thomas went into the autopsy room, and the heavy metal door whumped shut behind him; he didn't want the father to see his son as the lawmen had found him.

The few minutes that the sheriff had promised turned into forty-five, and each passing minute became tougher for Len Eberle to handle. Every once in a while a staff member would come out, perhaps pause briefly and look at him, then hurry away to attend to whatever business he or she had. Occasionally, someone would enter the room, and the whole process would be repeated in reverse.

The waiting wasn't as bad as the silence—and the stares that seemed to say: *"Oh. You're the father."*

"What the hell are they doing in there?" Len said to himself. "My God, can't we get this over with?"

Finally, the sheriff came out and led Len into the cold room. Immediately his eyes fell to the slightly tilted table in the center of the room. He was conscious of a faint humming sound, like air whispering from a vent somewhere.

The boy on the table seemed so small, so fragile. A solid white sheet was pulled up to his chin, and two round pieces of white cloth had been placed over his eyes.

For some strange reason, it bothered Len that he couldn't see the boy's eyes. He didn't need to see them; he had no doubt about who lay beneath the sheet. But still, it bothered him.

Danny Joe's always neatly-combed hair now appeared chopped in places. But Len Eberle sensed an aura of peace surrounding his son. The suffering was over now; Danny Joe could rest.

"We'll find whoever did this," Sheriff Thomas promised. "We'll get him."

Len Eberle didn't say anything as the sheriff led him from the room.

Judy Eberle could hear the sobs coming from the bedroom that her two youngest sons had shared. Through the partially open door, she could see Steve standing by the bed folding clothes. Not his own clothes; his big brother's. She watched him as he folded a shirt and laid it neatly on the bed. Then he folded a pair of pants and laid them beside the shirt. Judy pushed the door completely open. Quietly, she walked to her son and embraced him.

"What are you doing?" she whispered.

"I'm busy." His voice cracked with emotion. His lower lip trembled. "I want Danny to know I'm grown up."

Judy felt a twinge of heartsickness remembering how Danny Joe had often chastised Steve for not keeping his part of the room clean, for not keeping his clothes neatly folded and put in their place. No match for Danny Joe's perfection, young Steve had to take his medicine.

"Grow up!" Danny Joe used to tell his little brother. "When are you ever going to grow up?"

For a long time, Judy held her son, trying to calm him, trying to still his shaking, trying to tell him that everything would be all right. Then she realized that maybe she shouldn't encourage him to hold the hurt inside. So she hugged him one more time, got up, and quietly left the room. She could hear him sniffling behind her and, glancing back over her shoulder, could see the tears drying on his cheeks as he continued folding the clothes.

After his mother had gone, Steve looked around the room.

On the bookshelf, his brother's collection of matchbox cars sat immaculately in a row. Danny Joe had been so proud of those cars. Once, when his brother wasn't home, Steve had taken them to the basement.

He'd played at the foot of the stairs for several hours, first pretending to race one car against another, then playing crash-up derby.

Danny Joe had made it clear that these cars were not to be removed from their place on the shelf. Absolutely, positively, not under any conditions. But Steve was a little brother, and that meant often being left out of the fun he wanted so much to be part of. Well, if he weren't old enough to run with his brother's crowd, at least he could experience something close to his brother's heart.

After a while, the fun wore off, and sandy-haired Steve put all the cars back on the bookshelf. In his excitement, he hadn't noticed the tiny scratch he had managed somehow to rake down the side of his brother's favorite, the sleek black and silver sports car.

But Danny Joe noticed immediately.

"I told you never to mess with my cars," Danny Joe had fumed. "You've got your own."

With tears streaming from his eyes, Steve ran to his mother for comfort. But Mom sided with Danny Joe.

"You know those are Danny's cars," she said. "You know how he takes care of them. You've got your own toys."

She hugged him anyway until he stopped crying, then she sent him on his way.

The matchbox cars had been another lesson for Steve, and now, alone in a room full of memories, he finally realized it.

On the dresser were small framed pictures of Jesus and the Virgin Mary. Danny Joe was the most religious member of the family. Hardly a night passed that he didn't say his prayers, and despite occasional ribbing from his friends, he always wore a wooden cross on a chain around his neck. The cross was to remind him of Saint Anthony, his favorite saint. According to scripture, if you lost something and prayed to Saint Anthony, he would help you find it. Danny Joe had prayed to Saint Anthony many times, and usually whatever he had lost would turn up.

Again Steve began to cry. He knew that even Saint Anthony couldn't bring back his brother.

"I don't even know what to do," Len Eberle said as they drove to the mortuary the next morning.

"I'm sure someone will be there to help us," Judy said.

"How much should we spend?"

"Let's be reasonable. We can't afford something real expensive."

Len agreed. They would choose a simple casket. Something inexpensive, but not cheap.

By the time they arrived, however, they had begun to feel that price shouldn't be a consideration.

"I want something to give him his character back," Judy told her husband, "something to give him the respect he deserves."

At the mortuary, they got out of the car. Judy looked up at the big stone building. It was solemn, cold, uninviting. It made her feel uneasy. But as soon as she walked through the door, that impression changed.

Judy could not believe how pleasant it was inside, how warm the greeting. The viewing rooms were spacious and tastefully decorated in a way that made her relax. She felt as though the people there really cared about her family and their sadness.

"The casket room is downstairs," said the woman who met them. "Right this way."

Len and Judy followed her down the steps.

Judy sensed the sudden temperature change as they descended. Extreme cold, as if they had walked into a refrigerator. Was it really the temperature or just the empty, lonely feeling in her soul?

Whatever it was, she didn't like it.

"I'll let you look," the woman said, as she turned to go back upstairs.

Suddenly, the Eberles found themselves alone in the frigid room, alone except for the coffins of wood and of glistening steel.

My God, Judy thought. *This can't be happening. It can't be real. Look at all these stupid coffins.*

They walked about the room as if in a terrible dream. Within a few minutes they found what they wanted: a beautiful bronze casket. Judy touched the cool metal, ran her hand over the smooth surface. It seemed right, somehow. So sturdy and strong—like their son's personality.

"This is it," Judy said.

Their choice made, Leonard Eberle went to find the manager. They whispered together in the corner, Len assuring the man that somehow he would come up with the money to pay for the casket. Somehow he would find the money.

One decision down, there was another to make.

What should Danny Joe wear for the service? It didn't take his mother long to decide.

In the boy's bedroom closet, she found the pair of gray pants and the maroon shirt that he had bought just last month. It seemed like yesterday.

"I've found a neat-looking outfit over at K-Mart, Mom," he'd said one afternoon. *"Will you come with me to make sure it matches?"*

Danny Joe loved to shop at K-Mart, and he bought most of his own clothes there.

"Sure, son," Judy said. *"I'll go with you."*

It was just another reminder of how special her child had been. Very conscious of how others perceived him, wanting so much to make all the right decisions.

Another decision was made by Danny Joe's brothers and sisters.

"You have to give them a pair of his white socks," they told their mother. "He would have wanted it that way."

White socks had been Danny Joe's trademark. He could often be found handwashing three or four pairs of them at the kitchen sink. In addition to soap and water, he used his own special concoction of bleach. They had to be perfect. No matter how many times he'd worn them across the floor, there could be no sign of dirt on the soles.

"Don't touch those socks!" he'd call out to anyone who got near the mixture, and the family would break up laughing.

Judy found a brand new pair of socks in Danny Joe's drawer. Her eyes became misty as she turned them over in her hands. They were snow white and so soft. Later, at the mortuary, the manager promised that her son would be buried in them, and he kept that promise.

Danny Joe Eberle's funeral was held on Friday, September 23rd, at St. Mary's Catholic Church in Bellevue. It had been his favorite place of worship.

"Whoever did this might show up at the funeral," F.B.I. agent John Evans told the Eberles before the service. "We'll have agents inside the church, and someone outside taking pictures of people going in and out. That way there won't be any surprises, no one making an appearance who doesn't belong here. You may recognize some of the agents, but just pretend you don't know them."

Len and Judy nodded.

Judy paid little attention to the first part of the sermon; she was frustrated because the priest had not described Danny Joe's personality to her satisfaction. Her mind wandered, seemed to fade in and out of reality. The priest's voice seemed to reach her from a very great distance. She hoped that this was only a deep, ugly, dreadful dream. She felt as if she might wake up at anytime and find the sun streaming in the window and go downstairs to fix breakfast and get the kids off to school the way she did every morning.

Then the sick ache in her chest returned, and she knew that this was a dream from which she wouldn't awake. When the priest started to read letters from Danny Joe's classmates, Judy took a renewed interest in the service.

". . . he was the kind of guy who would give you his pencil if you didn't have one," a little boy had written.

"I want to see him, Dad," Lenny whispered to his father. "Make them open the casket."

Len shook his head and sighed; they had been over this the night before.

"It's a closed coffin funeral," his Dad whispered. "He's been beat up too bad."

But the explanation didn't satisfy Lenny. He wanted to prove the police wrong. He wanted to show them that his brother wasn't dead.

"I've got to see him," he insisted, his eyes moist.

The service was nearly over, and Judy found herself staring at her son's casket; only now did she notice the six inch crucifix on top.

Dear God, she prayed. *Please don't put me through this. Please don't let him give me that cross. Not here. I don't think I can make it up there.*

As if on cue, the priest stepped down to the casket and removed the cross. He approached Judy and respectfully handed it to her. Judy Eberle felt faint, as if the strain would crush her.

Please, God, just let this be over.

This time her prayer was answered. Danny Joe Eberle was taken to the cemetery and laid to rest.

After the service, the Eberle family went home. They sat around the dining room table with other family members, talking softly, drinking coffee, and eating cake that had been intended for Maria's birthday, which would be tomorrow.

Danny Joe and Maria had been very close, and after the service she didn't feel like mingling with the visiting relatives. So she went away to be alone. She knew that this would be one birthday she'd remember for the rest of her life.

Chantel, at the age of nine, was still too young to really understand what had happened to her brother. She went from relative to relative telling them what her mother had told her: Danny Joe was safe in heaven now, he was with God.

Watching Chantel warmed Judy's heart. She was a special child, adopted at the age of nine months. Four children had not been enough for the Eberles; they'd wanted another. Judy especially wanted another daughter, but the adoption process, she was told, could take years. Then they heard about an adoption plan for Vietnamese children and decided to work through it. To Judy and Len, nationality didn't matter; they just wanted a little girl to love.

Judy remembered that morning in May, 1975, when they had gone to the airport to pick up Chantel.

Excitement was thick in the air as the whole family piled into their green station wagon, the kind with the veneer paneling on the side. As usual, the oldest children fought over who would get the "secret seat," the fold up seat in the back end of the car; this seat was sunken just enough to provide a "hidden-away" feeling for the two people who could ride there. As usual, nine-year-old Maria lost the battle. As usual, her little brothers had ganged up on her, and she was forced to sit behind her parents where she spent the entire trip baby-sitting little Stevie.

It was a long way to Chicago's O'Hare Airport, and soon novelty gave way to boredom.

"Are we there yet, Dad?" one of the children would ask every few miles or so.

Eight hours and fifteen bathroom stops after leaving home, the green station wagon with the wooden veneer on the sides pulled up to the terminal.

It must be quite a sight, Judy thought, as they walked through the revolving doors. A real life version of "The Family Circus."

Every few feet the boys would stop at the huge glass windows to watch the big jetliners roar down the run-way and lift gracefully into the sky. Maria, however, was more interested in the people than the planes, and to Judy's embarrassment, she expressed this interest at the top of her lungs.

"Mommy!" she yelled, pointing to a lady who looked more like an exotic dancer than an airline passenger, "why does that lady have on so much makeup?"

"Shhhhh!" Judy scolded, trying hard not to laugh at the lady with the bright blue eye shadow.

Finally, they reached the gate where the Vietnamese children were to be brought in. The Eberles' little girl was named Chantel, and she was coming to America from a poor family in Vietnam. After her husband deserted her, Chantel's mother had tried to raise four children by herself, but it was difficult. She had walked fifteen miles to make sure that her daughter arrived safely at the adoption agency.

"Here they come!" one of the children called out as the babies were carried down the walkway. Their own eyes filled with wonder, the Eberle children—Maria, Lenny, Danny Joe, and Stevie—searched the faces of each arriving infant, trying to pick out the baby whose face they'd seen only in a photograph.

"Is that one ours?" Maria would ask as each baby was carried past. *"How about that one?"*

Seven-year-old Lenny had already formed a theory about where babies came from, but seeing all of these children shattered it; he now wondered on which airline he had arrived.

Just as they were beginning to get worried, Chantel appeared. Cuddled in the arms of her American escort, she was one of the last children off the plane. She wore a bright yellow outfit, a perfect contrast to her dark hair and complexion.

"Oh! Look at her!"

"She's so tiny!"

"Can we take her home now?"

"Can I hold her?"

The moment could not have been happier. The Eberle children, too young for prejudice, welcoming their new sister.

"She's having a little trouble with her new diet," the escort told Judy. *"You might want to keep her on Jello water for a while."*

Judy nodded as she took the baby into her arms, cuddled her for a few seconds, then handed her to her beaming dad.

Back at the hotel, the children took turns holding Chantel. They smiled at her, cooed, held her tiny hands in theirs, and kissed her.

Quick, time out for a photo. Click. Everyone smiling but Danny Joe, who stared out of the frame with a somber look on his face.

Danny Joe had been the only one to hold back, trying to adjust to the new situation. That was his way; always analyzing things until he was sure they would work out. But within a few days, four-year-old Danny Joe had taken Chantel under his wing. It was just one of the many signs that Danny Joe was mature for his age.

Now, eight years later, Chantel was saying good-bye to her brother much as he had said hello to her; not so sure what the future would hold, but trusting that there was a reason for what had happened.

Suddenly, the phone rang, breaking into Judy's reminiscence like an intruder. Sure that another neighbor was calling to offer condolences, she did not move to answer it.

The call had come barely half an hour after the family returned from the service. Len's sister, Carol, reached to answer it. Suddenly, she froze, and her face went blank as the man's raspy voice asked his cruel and heartless question:

"Can Danny Joe come out and play . . . ?"

Six

[Pettit] "My God . . . how do you wake up each
day? What do you have to live for?
[Joubert] "Leaving. Having my case overturned."
[Pettit] "That someday you'll get out?"
[Joubert] "What else?"
        (John Joubert, in our first interview)

East Lansing, Michigan
Monday, September 19, 1983

As soon as he read the message the clerk handed him
when he got back to his hotel, Special Agent Bob Ressler knew that somewhere something was wrong.

"Call Quantico Immediately," the message said.

A few minutes later he was on the phone to his boss
at the F.B.I. training academy in Virginia.

"Bob we've got a homicide out in Omaha that looks
a lot like the Johnny Gosch case. I'd like you on the
first plane out of there tomorrow."

"I'll be on it," Ressler said without hesitation.

As one of the country's leading experts on criminal
behavior, Bob Ressler had worked on at least a hundred
homicides, including the John Wayne Gacy case in Chicago and the Wayne Williams case in Atlanta. He'd been
in East Lansing helping give a seminar at his alma ma-
ter, Michigan State University. Since the mid-seventies

51

the Bureau had invested heavily in psychological profiling—studying crimes and trying to understand those who committed them.

The job waiting for him in Nebraska certainly didn't compare to some of the others as far as number of victims went, but Ressler knew how a single killing could sometimes terrorize a community. He hoped that he could prevent more killings.

The next morning Ressler packed early and left for the airport. Two hours and a stop in Chicago later his plane touched down in a cold gray Nebraska mist. Ressler had sorely underestimated a fall day in Omaha. Yesterday, the thermometer had scored a record high of ninety-one degrees; then a wind shift followed by a heavy rain had sent the temperature plummeting.

As Ressler stepped from the plane onto the tarmac, he was greeted by an icy gust out of the north. He shuddered and tried to pull his light fall suit more tightly about him. The wind whipped his greying brown hair about his head.

I may be an expert in predicting criminal behavior, Ressler thought wryly, but I'd do well to stay out of weather forecasting.

John Evans met Ressler inside the terminal and, on the ride to the command center, briefed his fellow investigator on the case.

"It's a paperboy," he said. "We found him bound with rope and stabbed to death. We don't have a murder weapon or much else to go on."

Ressler didn't need anyone to paint a picture for him; the early indications pointed to another Johnny Gosch. This time, however, the body had been found. He knew how important the Des Moines case had become and was anxious to get to work on the Nebraska case.

At the Bellevue police station, Evans led Ressler to

the small office he shared with Sheriff Thomas. Evans then showed him pictures of the victim and the crime scene. Quietly, Ressler sifted through the photos, studied how the boy's hands and feet were bound, examined the wounds, noted how the suspect had disposed of the body. The killer was obviously inexperienced; apparently not sure where the vital organs were located, he had stabbed at random. The boy's body had been dumped in a hurry, which showed that the crime had not been well-planned. It also suggested that the murderer had panicked, had wanted to hide the body and get out of there fast. After reviewing the autopsy results and visiting the crime scene, Bob Ressler filed his report:

UNSUB;
Danny Joe Eberle—Victim
Kidnapping—Murder
(00: OMAHA)

The circumstances of the disappearance and recovery of the victim's body indicate that the abduction and murder of the victim does not seem to be consistent in modus operandi with the mysterious disappearance of Johnny Gosch, which occurred in Des Moines, Iowa, approximately one year earlier. Although the circumstances of the abductions are similar, the fact that the Gosch victim's body was never found and that Eberle's body was found several days after the abduction in a remote area outside of Bellevue in a rather random and hurried manner, differentiates between the types of individuals who might have committed the two crimes.

Facts indicate that the Eberle victim may have been kept alive by the Unknown Subject for a period of time and the lack of abrasions from any rope or other type of ligature would indicate that the victim had been free during most of his period of captivity and only tied up just prior to his demise. This indicates that the killer or killers may have treated him somewhat well for that period of time indicating to him that he would be freed if he cooperated in possible sexual assault and even in photographing him during sex acts.

The killer of Danny Joe Eberle is undoubtedly a youthful white male in his late teens or early twenties and there is a distinct possibility that this individual may have known Eberle on a casual basis. Although he may not have known Eberle well, it is possible that Eberle may have known him by sight, at least enough to approach the Unknown Subject's vehicle and possibly even enter that vehicle voluntarily. There is a possibility that the Unknown Subject may have been accompanied by one or two other individuals, also white males, in the same age group. A re-creation of events indicates that Eberle, while delivering newspapers on his paper route, was encountered by one or more Unknown Subjects in a motor vehicle and that he was either enticed or forced into the vehicle, taken to another location where he was held for a period of several days, possibly sexually assaulted, and eventually killed by a knife assault. Visual examination of crime scene and autopsy reports indicates no gross sexual assault, however, based on the personality of the victim, it is a definite possibility that the victim's death may have come as a result of an attempted sexual assault whereby the victim may have fought his assailant to the point of being killed. Further, forensic evidence indicates that the victim was possibly moved several times after death and the abandonment of his body on a remote roadside several miles outside of Bellevue suggests that the killer may have panicked after killing the victim and had dumped the body rather than bury it or dispose of it in a more permanent manner.

The dumping of the body just off a lightly traveled road suggests that the killer may not have possessed sufficient strength to carry the body further into a wooded area. It also indicates his hasty attempt to dispose of a body and poor planning. Pebble indentations in the victim's body and a pebble located in the mouth of the victim indicates that he had been lying in another location after death and then transported to the final scene of disposal as there were no such pebbles at the final dumpsite. It was a possibility that the Unknown Subject was somewhat aware of the location of the dumpsite of the body and may have traveled this area many times previously.

Examination of evidence indicates that the killer (or killers) would be single and not overly educated, certainly not beyond that of the high school level. The employment would range from unemployed to employed in a rather menial and unskilled capacity, possibly blue collar in nature.

The main perpetrator would definitely have had a chronic sexual problem indicating deviance and bizarre sexual experiences throughout his life. He would likely be an avid reader of pornography and may have been involved in experiments of a bizarre nature throughout his adolescence. This experimentation could definitely involve animals and possibly forced sexual acts on younger children, both male and female.

Indications are that the killer would have been involved in recent stressful events in his life which might include breaking up with a girlfriend, losing a job, being dropped from school, or trouble with his im-

mediate family. Further, the individual may have been absent from his employment, if employed, for several days before and after the disappearance of Eberle.

In summary, the abduction and killing of victim Eberle indicates a poorly planned and rather spontaneous crime which suggests that the subject or subjects had encountered Eberle during the normal course of their travel throughout the city of Bellevue and are possibly local residents. The abduction probably took place without particular motive or planning which might reinforce the theory that more than one individual is involved. The circumstances of this crime are sufficiently different to the Des Moines, Iowa, case involving victim Johnny Gosch to suggest that the perpetrator of the Gosch abduction would be considerably older, possibly in his thirties, and that there is probably no connection between these two cases.

Later, at a round table discussion with the lead investigators, Ressler further explained his findings.

"There are a number of possibilities here," he said. "The killer simply panicked and dumped the boy off the side of the road, or he wanted the body to be found to send a message. We have to consider that he's trying to flaunt what he did to shock society.

"This person is very lonely. More than likely he has repressed homosexual tendencies and isn't quite sure how to deal with them. I think it's fair to say he could be involved in coaching, handicrafts, something to get him close to children. To this point it doesn't appear to be the work of a serial killer; his modus operandi shows a lack of sophistication."

Not overly educated, a blue collar worker, a loner, and likely to kill again. Police had their work cut out for them, but at least now they had a better idea of who they were looking for.

History would later prove Agent Bob Ressler wrong on one count; there was only one killer. Ressler also had been misled about a pebble being found in Danny Joe Eberle's mouth.

Several days later, lawmen discovered the remnants of an aquarium in an old barn. The pebbles that had once lined the bottom seemed to be a perfect match for the pebble found in Danny Joe's mouth. It had taken the investigators a weekend's worth of hard work to find those pebbles.

When the pathologist briefed members of the task force, he was compelled to confess that he had made a mistake: the pebble supposedly found in the Eberle boy's mouth had actually come from the mouth of another person; the results had been put into the wrong file.

The investigators were silent while the doctor explained what had happened. Some were shaking their heads in disbelief. It wasn't the first time they'd been led down a wrong trail, nor would it be the last. But the frustration was almost too much to bear.

Finally, the doctor finished. No one said anything at first. Then one summed up all of their disgust and frustration in one word:

"Fuck," he sighed as he walked away.

SEVEN

*"Whoever did this is sick and needs help. He
should turn himself in to either a doctor, a priest,
or myself."*
(Sheriff Pat Thomas, trying to talk to the killer
through the media)

A major break in the case came one week after the
Eberle murder.

Police had picked up eighteen-year-old Alvin Terry*
for allegedly molesting two young boys; he had supposedly tied them up then sexually assaulted them. But
Terry denied any connection to Danny Joe's murder.

"I ain't your man," Terry told investigators. "Hey,
I fucked with these other kids, but I ain't never killed
nobody, and I ain't going to. I went fishing that morning."

"You got a girl friend?" one of his interrogators
asked.

"Not no more," Terry said. "I had one. We had fun.
I'm not gay or nothing."

"Why did you assault these boys then?"

None of your fucking business, Terry thought.

"I don't know," he said. "I guess I'm sick in the
head. Just got fucking problems."

Where did they get off bugging him like this? He

---

*Alvin Terry is a fictitious name used for this person.

58

wasn't a killer, and he'd told them so. But behind his bold, brown eyes there were secrets he wasn't about to share with the police, such as what had happened to him several years before on a weekend camping trip. Some of the older boys had grabbed him and pulled down his pants. They'd tied his feet together, had thrown the other end of the rope over a tree limb, and had hoisted him up. Then, while he was hanging upside down, helpless, they had slapped at his penis and bare buttocks.

"Give him a pink belly!" one of the boys ordered.

Another boy slapped Terry again and again across the stomach while the others cackled in unison.

Alvin Terry felt as though he were being raped. He was mortified. There were adults along on this trip, and Terry could see them standing some distance away, could hear them laughing. What were they just standing there for? They were supposed to look after the younger boys. Weren't they? Why didn't they do something?

Alvin Terry didn't cry. He held the hurt, the humiliation, and the tears inside him. He had a score to settle, and he would try to settle it on many occasions. The daily beatings his older brother gave him also helped erode his self-esteem and fuel his rage.

Sure, maybe he was guilty of abusing young boys, but he'd never killed anyone.

Terry agreed to a polygraph test in order to clear himself. During the test, Bob Ressler watched the teenager closely. Terry was shaking, and his eyes were darting from side to side. He was a total nervous wreck. Ressler slipped out of the room to talk to John Evans.

"Polygraph over with?" John Evans asked.

"No."

"What do you think?"

"If it's not him," Ressler said, "it's someone just like him."

Evans wondered how someone like Terry could be on the streets. Picking him up, however, had served two purposes: 1) if Terry was involved in the Eberle case, he was now out of circulation, and 2) if he wasn't involved, his arrest at least proved to the public that the police were doing their job.

A few hours later, the polygraph test results were back, and Alvin Terry had failed. It wouldn't be the first time he had lied to interrogators; he'd lied about being with a friend on the day one of the other boys had been assaulted.

"You're not telling us the truth, Alvin," one of the officers said.

"Okay, man. I lied about that. It's called covering your ass. That's the buddy system. It's called being friends."

"Yeah," said another investigator, "and what happened to Danny Joe Eberle is called murder."

"I told you, man," Terry whined, "you got the wrong guy!"

"You won't mind if we take a few hair samples then, will you?"

A few minutes later, Terry was handed three small combs.

"Run one through your hair," the officer instructed, "one under your arms, the other through your pubic hair."

Terry obeyed. Each comb was sealed in a separate plastic pouch, labelled, and sent to the crime lab.

A search of Terry's house turned up more damning evidence: rope, tape, a knife. Investigators talked to people who knew Terry; many described him as a young man with a lot of problems, a person who at times was violent, a smoldering firecracker who could be set off by the least little thing.

The F.B.I. crime lab in Washington was ordered to

give the Eberle case top priority, and soon reports came back on evidence found at the scene. The boy had not been sexually assaulted, the lab discovered, and he may have lived for a short time after being left in the field. One thing still puzzled investigators, however. There had been a rainstorm the day before Danny Joe Eberle's body had been found. Although it had been a soaking rain, the boy's clothes were completely dry—further evidence that the killer may have kept him alive for some time before killing him.

A few days later, more information arrived.

"The lab says it's 99% sure," Lieutenant Sanderson told Sheriff Thomas and Agent Evans, "that the hair found on the boy's body matches one from Alvin Terry's head."

"I think we've got our man," Thomas said.

But Sanderson felt uneasy.

"It doesn't make any sense," he said, looking at his friend from the F.B.I. "This isn't in his league. I mean, Terry's a two-bit faggot. I just don't think he did it."

"I feel the same way," Evans said. "But God, Jim. This guy's starting to fit the picture."

After this discussion, Evans walked back to the cell block to talk to Terry. Again Terry claimed he was innocent.

"You know, Alvin," Evans said. "I believe you. I don't think you killed this kid. But if this were the Old West, we'd be getting ready to hang you."

The pressure was building. They could all feel it. A week into the case, and the public wanted action. The last thing the task force needed was a mistake.

The seven department heads from each of the law enforcement agencies working on the case—Sheriff Thomas, Police Chief Warren Robinson, John Evans and Agent Chuck Kempf from the Bureau, Captain Don Carlson, Lieutenant Jim Sanderson, and Captain Dan

Jackson—gathered in a conference room at Bellevue Police Headquarters.

"Okay," Sheriff Thomas sighed, leaning forward in his chair. "We all know the facts here. The crime lab says a hair found on the Eberle body matches that of Alvin Terry. He's failed a polygraph, admits attacking two other boys, and frankly doesn't know where the hell he was the day Danny Joe went missing. Chief Robinson, John Evans, and I think we should vote on this. We'll start at this end of the table. I say yes, we charge him."

Chief Robinson agreed.

"I know it doesn't all add up," the chief said, his face taking on a bewildered expression. "But what else do we have?"

"I have a gut feeling that Terry isn't the guy," Chuck Kempf said, glancing around the table for support.

"I agree with Chuck," Sanderson said. "It's like putting a round pin in a square hole. It goes in but just doesn't fit. Look, we all know Terry's background. He's queer, but I don't think he's a killer."

"Bullshit!" Thomas exploded. "Maybe I should go in there and get Terry to tell the truth. It's obvious somebody hasn't done their job. Basic policework. How tough is it?"

"You're about to make a fucking mistake," Sanderson shot back at his boss. "Then what do we do?"

The argument was becoming heated, but it pleased Thomas to see how well his young lieutenant was handling the job. Voting continued around the table; when it was over, three said charge Terry, four said no. Another polygraph test was ordered, and this time Terry passed. Investigators decided not to charge him.

Alvin Terry had literally come within a hair of being charged with a murder he didn't commit.

From that point on, every potential suspect received

the "Terry Treatment." Each person's alibi was checked and double checked. If he said he'd gone fishing, investigators found out what fishing hole, who'd gone with him, what they'd talked about, if anyone else remembered seeing them—everything about the alleged fishing trip down to what they'd used for bait.

Once again they went back to the psychological profile. Bob Ressler had pointed out that Danny Joe Eberle's killer probably had trouble relating to women and most likely never had sex with a woman. So the "Pervert Squad" was formed to find and interrogate every known sexual deviant. It seemed an easy enough task, but no one foresaw how long that list would become. It began with known sex offenders like Alvin Terry and grew to include names like Kenyon Ellis*— Major Kenyon Ellis, U.S. Air Force.

When the sun went down, Major Ellis became Cadillac Ken. Many a night he could be found cruising "The Run," an area in downtown Omaha where young boys slip quietly through the shadows and into cars with men like Ellis where they do things they're ashamed to talk about when daylight returns.

Major Ellis was a rough-looking but handsome man of forty-three. He had short brown hair, strong facial features, and eyes that seemed to bore into your soul when he looked at you. His predilection for young boys had shattered his marriage and gotten him booted out of the service. Investigators in the Eberle case found several boys who admitted letting Cadillac Ken perform sex acts on them.

"Why'd you do it?" one boy was asked.

"I was afraid he'd kill me if I didn't."

So Major Ellis became a prime suspect.

The Major had a way with boys. He targeted those

---

*Kenyon Ellis is a fictitious name used for this person.

from broken homes, those he knew to be in need of a role model. Boys with alcohol and drug problems were also fair game. Major Ellis was very supportive, very sympathetic. Once they had come to trust him, he would turn their dependency against them; he'd provide what they needed only if they would give him what he needed.

Sometimes, as in the case of Ian Keller,* it started innocently enough.

"I got a terrible sunburn while cutting the grass," the fifteen-year-old had complained one night at Ellis's home. "It really itches."

"I tell you, Ian," the major said, "I've got some lotion in the closet. It might help. Come on back to my room."

Naively, the boy followed Ellis to his bedroom.

"Take off your shirt and lie down on the bed. I'll be glad to rub it on for you."

A little embarrassed, Ian pulled his T-shirt over his head. His back was very red and tender. Gently, he eased himself down on the bed, which jiggled under his weight.

Ellis squeezed some lotion into his palm and knelt down by the bedside. Ian flinched at the cold touch of the Major's fingers.

"Just be still. . . ."

Ellis's voice was soothing, comforting. His hands moved in slow, gentle, caressing circles on Ian's back. Ian's muscles began to relax. Excitement was pumping through the Major's body as he massaged Ian's back, then up over his shoulder blades. His touch lingered for a moment on the boy's frail shoulders. Then he continued making the small circles.

"How's that feeling?" he asked softly.

*Ian Keller is a fictitious name used for this person.

"Really good."

Ellis's hands moved lower on the boy's back.

"Wouldn't it be nice," he whispered, "to have a good-looking woman doing this for you?"

"Sure would," Ian said, his eyes tightly closed, as if he were dreaming. "It sure would be nice."

Ellis could see that the boy was becoming sexually excited. He picked up the tube of lotion and squeezed some more into his hand.

"She'd probably do a lot more for you than this."

Ian lay quietly on the bed, his back arched slightly, one leg drawn up a little above the other one on the covers. Slowly, Ellis rubbed the lotion into the boy's skin. The Major's eyes seemed to do as much caressing as his hands.

"Just relax. . . ." he whispered, not unlike the hypothetical woman might whisper. Once more, his hands slipped to Ian's midsection. Discretely, his right hand touched the waistband of the boy's loosely-fitting jeans. "Just enjoy it."

Suddenly, Ellis slid his hand inside Ian's pants and clutched his erection.

The boy jerked away. He rolled over and stood up, glaring at Ellis across the bed.

"What're you doing, man! You fucking queer—don't touch me again!"

This caught the major off guard, but he didn't let it show.

"I'm sorry, Ian. My hand slipped."

"Like hell, man! Don't you fucking come near me. I should call the cops."

"Yeah, you do that," Ellis said coldly. His eyes narrowed, and Ian felt as if they were looking through him. He shivered, feeling naked before this man. "Just you go ahead and call the cops. I'm sure they'll believe a trouble-making punk like you!"

Ian picked up his shirt, flung it over his shoulder, and backed out of the room.

This time Cadillac Ken had misjudged his prey, but he didn't let it bother him. More than a dozen times before he'd gotten what he wanted. Ian wouldn't go to the police. Ellis was sure of that. The kid would be too embarrassed. Besides, how would he explain getting into the situation in the first place?

But Ian Keller did go to the police, and the investigation that followed turned up others whom Ellis had abused. Eventually, the major would plead guilty to two counts of sexually assaulting young boys; then, in the confusion, he would manage to slip through the cracks in the judicial system. So far, Major Kenyon Ellis has not served one minute in prison for his crimes.

Then there was Nick Buttress,* a balding, forty-year-old, overweight homosexual. He used a camera to carry out his schemes.

"This chick's hot for you guys," he told the two boys sitting in the living room of his apartment. "It's just a matter of which one she picks."

One of the boys was fourteen, the other fifteen. Both were grinning from ear to ear. Buttress could see that his revelation had excited them.

"So . . . why don't you guys strip down to your underwear, give me your best pose, and I'll get a photo for her. I'll take the pictures over to her place tonight, and tomorrow I'll let you know who she chose."

The boys eagerly shed their clothes and struck up their best "muscle man" poses for the man they thought was their friend.

Looking through the viewfinder, Buttress drooled over their ripe young bodies.

*Nick Buttress is a fictitious name used for this person.

Shhhk. Shhhk. Shhhk.

Shot after shot in rapid succession, the camera's motor drive whisking the film from one frame to the next.

"Just one more. . . ."

Shhk.

"That's great. Let's get another. . . ."

Shhhk. Shhhk.

"O.K." Buttress said finally. "I think we've got enough. See you guys tomorrow."

The next day, the boys were back.

"Man," Buttress said. "This woman is hot, but she can't make up her mind. She likes both of you and says it depends on who's got the biggest *thing*. She wants me to take some more pictures for her."

The fourteen-year-old frowned skeptically.

"I don't know, Nick. . . ."

"Hey, it's up to you guys. You make the decision: do you want to get laid or not?"

The boys looked at each other, uncertain what to say next.

"Let's do it and get it over with," the fifteen-year-old said.

Slowly they removed their clothing, everything but their underpants. After a hesitation, they pulled those off, too.

"She's got to see you hard, guys. Let's go."

Their faces and shoulders flushed, the boys began to fondle themselves. The camera clicked, and the strobe light flashed.

Shhhk. Shhhk. Shhhk.

"All right," Buttress said, lowering the camera. "That should do it. Tomorrow's the big day. See you then."

But when they returned the next day, Buttress had a confession to make.

"I've got to be honest with you," he said. "There ain't no girl."

"What!" the fifteen-year-old yelled, his eyes flaring in anger. "What do you mean 'no girl'?"

"What I mean," Buttress said, his voice taking on a hard edge, "is that I don't think you'd like your parents to see those pictures, and if you don't do what I tell you, I'll make sure that they do see them."

"You bastard!" the fifteen-year-old exploded.

But they were helpless. Under no circumstances could their parents ever see those photos, so the boys were forced to have sex with Buttress. When police finally caught on to him, they found an album full of nude photographs of young boys.

The list of deviants grew.

One man had paid a youngster $800 to urinate on him and had offered to give another a new car if he would do the same.

A lot of those who made the "pervert list" were older men, men in their fifties. Men like Art Meloy.*

Using his farm for a cover and easy money for a lure, Meloy hired teenagers to work for him. When they found themselves short of cash, "Uncle Art" could always be found with checkbook in hand. At first, he never asked for anything in return. He didn't even ask that the loans be paid back. That is, not until he had the boys sufficiently indebted to him; then he would ask for sexual favors. Usually he got them. If he didn't, the loans would stop.

But Meloy—like many others on the "pervert list"— finally fell victim to the Eberle spin-off investigation; one of his young victims had had the courage to turn him in. Like Major Ellis, Art Meloy would draw probation instead of a prison sentence, but unlike the Ma-

---

*Art Meloy is a fictitious name used for this person.

jor, Meloy wouldn't live to serve out his term. During one hot Nebraska summer, he would collapse and die of a heart attack on the same farm where he had tricked young boys into doing things of which they were ashamed.

The "Pervert Squad" turned up 2,800 names. Each person questioned would lead police to four or five others just like him but investigators turned up nothing that would help them with the Eberle case. Finally, Sheriff Thomas had to go before the television cameras and tell the people of his county that he was no closer than he'd ever been to finding the man responsible for killing Danny Joe Eberle.

John Joubert smiled as he watched Thomas on the evening news. He wasn't concerned. The lawmen had nothing to go on, and he knew it. They weren't even close to finding him. It was all working the way it should work. And why not? He had been planning this since he was six years old.

EIGHT

*"She's my last hope in here [prison]. That some-
where, sometime, someone liked me."*
*(John Joubert, remembering the girl he had a
crush on at the age of 12)*

Lawrence, Massachusetts
1969

These weren't the best of times for the Joubert family. Six-year-old John did not understand why his father
slept on the couch, nor did he know why his mother
was spending more and more time talking with her
friend.

"He's no good," the friend said. "Take the kids and
leave."

Leaving would not be easy for Beverly Joubert. In a
Catholic family, divorce wasn't a subject discussed at
the dinner table.

Beverly was a stern-faced woman, a hard worker, a
bookkeeper; it was no secret that she wore the pants in
the Joubert household. Her husband Jack had spent most
of his adult life in the restaurant business. For many
years, his parents had operated Joubert's Diner. When
it closed, Jack doubled as cook and waiter at another
small cafe. He wasn't the role model Beverly wanted
for their children.

John and his sister Jane spent many hours in the care of a sitter. They were lonely hours. John spent them wishing for his parents to come home, wishing that they wouldn't yell at each other so much.

Soon John grew to hate the sitter and her mother. The sitter's mother was the same friend who had advised his mother to leave his father. He felt they were part of some strange conspiracy to break up his family. It didn't take long for his hate to evolve into thoughts of murder. He would daydream about killing his babysitter; not a brutal murder, but a clean kill—if there could be such a thing.

"Like turning off a light switch," he would say later, "and she would be gone."

Never during this time did he tell anyone about his bizarre fantasies. Every day they would become more and more realistic. The pretty young girl would be lying dead on the floor, and he would kneel down beside her and eat her body. These fantasies confused him; he didn't know why his mind was full of thoughts about murder and cannibalism. All he knew was that, in some strange way, he liked them.

John longed to fit in with the other kids at school. He joined the Cub Scouts and took part in all their activities. But not even wearing the blue uniform with the yellow necktie to school on meeting days, like all the other scouts, made him part of the "in crowd." He still felt like an outcast.

In 1971, Beverly Joubert had had enough. Since the house belonged to Jack's parents, she had no choice but to move. John, his five-year-old sister, and his mother were crowded into a cramped, run-down apartment in a run-down three-story building. John didn't like his new home; to him, it was a rat trap.

John's situation at school had deteriorated, too. He was smaller than most of the other boys and skinny enough so you could count every rib. Many of the other kids ignored him. Others teased him because of his size and because he was not "one of them." Although his grades were good, the teacher had printed on his report card: DOES NOT PLAY WELL WITH OTHER CHILDREN.

One thing John did like about school was playing "Relievo" at recess. In Relievo, the players are divided into two teams. Each team has a territory to maintain, but it wants to expand. So it tries to capture members of the other team and hustle them back to its own territory; the team capturing the most players wins the game. John's size made him an easy target, and he wasn't an aggressive hunter. The thing he liked about Relievo was evading those out to get him; that he did very well.

John Joubert still despised his babysitter and her mother, both strict enforcers of a rule he didn't understand: although his father lived just across the street from the sitter, John and his sister were not allowed to visit him.

"You can go see your friends down the block," the sitter would tell him. "But don't go over to your father's house."

"Why not?"

"Because your mother says so."

John felt that his mother was too demanding. For one thing, she monitored his television viewing carefully and wouldn't let him watch shows that she thought were too violent. She expected him to be home by 9 P.M. every night, and once she'd told him that he would have to get a job and help with expenses at home. Later, he would have to work himself through high school, and his mother wouldn't let him get his driver's license when he was sixteen like most of the boys he knew.

In 1974, his mother announced that they were mov-

ing to Portland, Maine. Again the family would be up-
rooted. Considering where they'd ended up after leaving
his father, John didn't know if he could handle the fear
and uncertainty of another move.

Portland, a city of approximately 60,000 people, lies
along the Atlantic coast just south of Lewiston. It's pri-
marily a blue collar town where most of the residents
work in the lumber mills, paper mills, or leather fac-
tories. Portland is a city of character. Brick sidewalks
can still be found, and Victorian homes still line the
narrow streets. A town of Puritan values where the Sab-
bath is faithfully observed, and 80% of the stores are
closed on Sunday.

In his new town, John was lonely and bored. He was
tired of moving, and he didn't like the way his mother
told him to do this or that or told him not to do this or
that. He wondered if things could possibly get any
worse.

"I want to live with Dad," he said to her one day.

"Sure, do that," his mother said, "and you'll end
up in a public school."

Although John was now attending a public grade
school, Beverly Joubert wanted her son to attend the
all-boys Catholic high school in Portland.

"Your father has a hard enough time supporting that
woman he's married to now," she told him. "He certainly won't be able to come up with a thousand dollars
a year for tuition."

So John remained in Portland.

The way he looked at it, at least their new home was
better than the last place. Another family shared the
two-story frame house with them, but there was still
plenty of room. John especially liked the big backyard
which adjoined another lot which had several trees for
a boy to climb. An old oak split in two by a bolt of

lightning provided John with many afternoons of fun. Still, he missed his father who was a good ninety miles away.

John Joubert now attended Nathan Clifford Elementary School, just a few blocks from home. A beautiful three-story, blonde brick building constructed in 1907, Nathan Clifford was the epitome of character and class in Portland.

John's favorite teacher was Fred Bradbury. A slight man with graying hair and matching wire-frame glasses, Mr. Bradbury loved his job. He'd been an educator for almost twenty years, had taught high school, had even been a principal, but he especially liked working with younger children. "The Sixth Grade Syndrome," he called it, that period of life when the youngsters were becoming young men and women. They needed a teacher most at this time, someone to help mold them, help prepare them for adulthood. Many an afternoon at recess, Fred Bradbury would stand on the playground and watch the children playing kickball. His heart would ache every time he saw John Joubert step up to the plate.

"Oh, no," one of John's teammates would yell. "Here's another out!"

Others would take up the call. John's face would grow red, his jaw become rigid, but he wouldn't back down. He did his best, but usually his classmates' predictions came true.

Like most teachers, Mr. Bradbury tried at times to make predictions of his own. He tried to envision what this student would become, what that student would do. One girl in his class, for instance, would surely be a teacher someday, and there was this other boy who would certainly become captain of the football team.

But John Joubert worried him. Mr. Bradbury was more concerned about what John was at that moment than what he would eventually become. He tried to offer encouragement whenever he could.

"It's okay, John," he would say, "you'll kick the ball next time."

Fred Bradbury liked classroom experiments. He had one of those old telephones with the crank that he'd rigged to generate electricity. That telephone could generate enough electricity to light a light bulb, Mr. Bradbury's favorite demonstration.

"Let's have you five form a line here," Mr. Bradbury said one afternoon, motioning to the row by the blackboard.

Desks creaked and shoes scuffed on the floor tiles as the kids got up and moved to the front of the room. A whispering arose from those still seated.

"Now join hands."

Jimmy Walker stood in front. Mr. Bradbury gave him a light bulb and told him to hold it about shoulder high, then he told the girl at the end of the line to crank the phone.

"Those of you watching," Mr. Bradbury said, "be sure to stand back from those in line. If you touch them, you'll act as the ground, and the person you touch will get a shock."

Jimmy Walker, known as "Butch" to his classmates, was bigger than most of the kids and extremely popular. John Joubert envied him. At times, he wanted to be more like Jimmy. But that could never happen. He would never be as big as Jimmy, never as well-liked. No matter what Joubert did, his classmates laughed at him or teased him or just plain did not want him around.

Well, if he couldn't be like Jimmy, he could at least get even with the show-off.

As the experiment neared its climax, John stepped forward and touched Jimmy Walker's elbow. A short pop. Butch Walker jerked.

"Ouch!" he yelped. "What the hell are you doing?"

"John!" Mr. Bradbury yelled. "I told you not to do that."

Without saying a word, John slunk back to his seat as quiet laughter blossomed in the room.

Like most boys his age, John was soon bitten by the oldest of bugs. At the age of twelve he found himself in love. The girl's name was Debbie Foster, an eleven-year-old with long brown hair that flowed like a river down over her shoulders. To John, she was the most beautiful girl in class. He was overjoyed one day when Mr. Bradbury arranged their desks in a "U" shape, and he wound up sitting just across the aisle from Debbie. He even started to think she liked him. Still, there was never any of that puppy love correspondence that usually takes place between youngsters who are attracted to each other: I LOVE YOU, DO YOU LOVE ME? CHECK YES OR NO.

John never could bring himself to send one of those notes. What if Debbie sent it back with the NO box checked?

Once he got to play the lead opposite her in a short skit from their *Weekly Reader*. It was a story from the television show *Little House on the Prairie*. Mr. Bradbury chose John to play the father, Charles Ingalls, and he tapped Debbie for the role of Caroline, the mother.

It was both a dream come true and a nightmare. He wanted so much to be close to the little brown-haired girl, but he couldn't let anyone else know how he felt. He would die if anyone suspected.

Despite his fears, he gave a good performance, and no one guessed his true feelings. For a while he felt as if he were actually on the television show with its contented family and happy ending. But unlike Charles and Caroline Ingalls, John and Debbie could never live happily ever after. Soon one question—a question that would have been brushed off by most of the other boys in class—changed things forever:

"Are you gay?" Jimmy Walker asked one day at recess.

He looked John Joubert straight in the eyes, waited for a reaction. The question confused John. Where he had come from, "gay" meant happy or jolly. Why would Jimmy Walker suddenly ask him that and look at him as if being gay were some big deal?

"Yes," he said without thinking. "I'm gay."

Jimmy Walker couldn't believe his ears. He stared at John, then burst out laughing and ran toward the school building.

"Hey," he called to one of his friends, "you know what Joubert just said. . . ."

Word spread like a disease through the school.

John Joubert. . . . You know? The skinny little guy who couldn't kick a home run to save his life? He admitted that he's a homosexual.

John was devastated. Debbie Foster would hear the rumor, he just knew it. The way the other kids were whispering behind his back, she couldn't avoid hearing it. She never confronted him, but neither did she try to be more than just his friend. Through junior and senior high school, the rumor continued to haunt him. John was a loner by nature, and that gave his classmates added fuel for speculation. He had a few successes, such as making Eagle Scout when he was seventeen, but people didn't talk about his accomplishments. No. What good were achievements when you could gossip about a person instead? So John Joubert drew further into his shell.

The hurt stayed with him. He winced every time he heard people talking in low voices, every time someone glanced at him in a curious way. He was sure they were talking about him.

All through high school, John kept to himself. He
had only one real date—to his prom. It was more a date
of convenience, really, than of attraction. He hadn't even
kissed her good night, and to this day he has never had
sex with a woman.

The hurt was like an open sore, festering inside him,
eating away his flesh, cutting deeper and deeper until
he thought he would go insane.

NINE

4:05 P.M., December 11, 1979

Nine-year-old Sarah Canty didn't see the dark-haired boy on the green ten-speed bike coming up fast behind her. She was more concerned with retrieving the football that she had dropped. The football had bounced and tumbled awkwardly before coming to rest in the grass beside the sidewalk. As she bent down to grab it, the bicycle sped past just a few feet from her. Confused, Sarah started to stand up.

Sarah screamed at the shooting pain in her back. She didn't see the broken pencil fall to the sidewalk, bounce and roll the way her football had bounced and rolled. She didn't care about the boy on the green ten-speed who had kept on riding. Her back was on fire. Crying hysterically, Sarah ran indoors to seek comfort from her mother and father.

Sarah gave a good description of her attacker, but the police could not find the boy. There were no fingerprints on the pencil. There were no witnesses to the assault, either. The quarter-inch puncture wound in Sarah's back soon healed, but it would be years before anyone learned that the boy on the bike had been John Joubert, and that Sarah Canty had not been his first victim. She had been his third.

The bus wheezed to a stop, the doors swung open, and John Joubert stepped out onto the sidewalk. He was on his way home from the public library where he worked. It had been snowing off and on for most of that cold October day, and snow was still coming down.

Almost as soon as Joubert's foot touched the sidewalk, he saw the boy walking alone down the street. He studied the boy for a moment, then as the bus puffed away from the curb, John Joubert fell into step behind the youngster.

The Maine National Bank sits on the corner of Forest and William, one of the busiest intersections in town. But that didn't bother Joubert; his mind was focused only on the boy.

"Hey," Joubert called. "Wait a minute."

The boy turned around, but he didn't speak. Instead, he turned into the bank's parking lot and stopped under the awning of the drive-in entrance where he waited for Joubert to catch up.

John Joubert was amazed at how easy it had been to get the boy's attention and to stop him.

"What's your name?"

"Chris Day."

"How old are you?"

"Eight," the boy said impatiently, frowning. "What do you want from me?"

Grabbing the boy's throat, Joubert shoved him against the building. The pavement was slick with ice, the brick wall cold against Chris Day's back. The boy tried to struggle, but John Joubert's gloved hands tightened, squeezing his windpipe so that Chris couldn't breathe. His face was turning red, and his head throbbed with every beat of his heart. Panicked, he swung his arms wildly. Suddenly he was loose and running awkwardly down the street, trying not to slip on the ice and fall. If he fell it would be all over.

Joubert watched him go. He was bigger than the boy, could easily have caught him. But there would be another chance.

That chance came a month later.

Usually Joubert searched for victims while delivering his morning papers, but he spotted his next prospect on the way home from school.

A girl between the ages of seven and nine. At first he didn't realize she was a girl. She was so bundled up against the cold that it was hard to tell.

"Hey," Joubert called.

The girl stopped, turned around, looked him over uncertainly. Joubert motioned to her.

"Come here."

"Why?"

"I want to talk to you."

The light wind made a soft rushing sound through the skeletal tree branches. Not far away was the back door of the Kentucky Fried Chicken restaurant, and Joubert could smell the food cooking. In the distance, he heard sounds of the city. An occasional beep of a car horn. A car's engine turning over. Once, he might have heard voices, faintly, but he couldn't be sure.

But here among the trees was only snow and the wind making that lonely sound through the branches.

"Are you going to take me home?" the child asked innocently.

She was not afraid, either, just as Chris Day had not been afraid. Joubert was startled at her lack of fear.

"I have a doctor's appointment," she said. "I have to go."

"Go ahead," John Joubert said, not quite sure why he said it.

Calmly, the girl turned and continued on her way. Joubert watched until she was out of sight. Then he headed for home.

Joubert was not discouraged. The first two were just for practice. He could find another victim, and next time he'd be more successful. The next day, from the fourth floor kitchen of the library where he worked, John Joubert stole a knife.

6:35 P.M., January 24, 1980.

Vicky Goff had always dreamed of becoming a teacher, and now, at the age of twenty-seven, her dream was coming true. She was on her way to class at the University of Maine when, shortly after turning onto Deering Avenue, she noticed a young man walking toward her along the street lined with middle class frame houses.

She had no inkling that something was different about this man. No sixth sense warned her away. As they both neared the intersection, she noted how thin he was, and short, perhaps 5'5" or 5'6". His tan coat was zipped up to the bottom of his neck, and he wore a light-colored cap with dark hair sticking out from under it.

They passed without words. A few seconds later, she heard someone running behind her. She glanced over her shoulder. The man slowed to a rapid walk. He crossed the street and came up beside her. He made her uncomfortable, keeping pace with her and not saying anything.

"Hello," she said. "Cold out tonight, isn't it?"

The man said nothing. He quickened his pace and walked ahead of her. Vicky Goff thought the young man's behavior rather odd, but she didn't feel threatened.

As she neared the university, Vicky again heard footsteps clicking on the sidewalk behind her. First slow, then faster and faster. Vicky started to turn. Suddenly, a mittened hand clamped over her mouth and nose, and she heard a sound like a knife being thrust into the earth. A moment later, she felt the sting in her right lung. Pain blossomed out from that point until it raged like a fire out of control. The woman gasped and pitched forward onto her knees. Clutching at her back, Vicky looked up into the face of the man who had passed her earlier, a face devoid of any emotion.

Vicky Goff somehow stumbled to her feet and ran. She turned up the walk of the first house she came to. Frantic, she hammered on the door, tears drying like trails of ice on her face, breathing in heaving, sobbing gasps, breath billowing out in frosty white puffs that swirled away like the smoke of a cigar. And somewhere inside her, down deep in her chest, the hurt, the throbbing, aching hurt. . . .

"Please help me!" she screamed.

There was someone inside. An elderly man. She could see him through the window in the door, could hear him shift slightly. But he would not open up.

"Please! I've been stabbed! Please help me!"

Still the elderly man didn't open the door.

Open up, she thought wildly. *Please! I'm hurt. I may be dying. I'm going to bleed to death right on your front porch. Please, open up!*

Finally, she gave up. She had calmed down considerably. If she kept her wits about her, she would not bleed to death on this old man's front porch. She would not bleed to death anywhere if she could help it.

Suddenly a wave of weakness slammed into her, and she swayed.

You must not faint, she thought. *If you faint, you may not wake up*.

Carefully, she made her way down from the porch. With every step, the fire flared up in her chest. She looked toward the university. Her decision made, she began walking. There she would find the help she needed.

Later, John Joubert lay in bed listening to the news on his radio. He smiled when the announcer mentioned the young coed who had been attacked on her way to night classes at the university. The knife had punctured her stomach cavity. She was in serious condition but resting comfortably; she would live. Joubert wasn't worried. He gathered from the radio account that the police had no clues. There were hundreds, perhaps thousands, of young men who fit the description given by the Goff woman. Why would they single him out? Surely, he was safe.

Joubert was on his way home from school two days later when the police cruiser pulled up beside him. The officer rolled down his window. He crooked his finger and motioned to Joubert. The teenager stepped over to the cruiser's door.

"A lady was attacked near here a couple nights ago," the officer said. "We're trying to find people who might've been in the area."

There was a fluttery feeling inside Joubert, as if his chest were full of moths. He tried not to let the officer see his nervousness.

"What's your name?" the officer asked.

"John Joubert."

"Where do you live?"

"Just down the road," he said, pointing.

"Okay. Thanks for your help."

Was it that easy? Was that all there was to being

questioned for a crime? They'd never catch him if that was all they did. John Joubert felt superior to the officer, and safer than ever.

March 24, 1980.

Nine-year-old Michael Witham was bundled up for the cold. It had snowed that day, and snow still lay glistening on lawns and rooftops and piled in drifts along sidewalks and streets where it had been shovelled or plowed aside. As he was passing the Temple Beth-El in one of the nicer sections of the city, he heard someone call to him.

Michael stopped, listened, glanced around. Then he spotted the older boy, standing at the top of the hill across the street. When he saw Michael looking, he waved.

"Hey!" the older boy yelled. "Come here!"

"What?"

"Come here!"

Michael Witham hesitated only a moment. Then he went across the street and started up the hill. Once or twice, his foot slipped in the snow, and he almost fell, but soon he reached the top.

"What?"

"Where do you live?"

"Way down there," Michael said, pointing toward Dartmouth Street.

"What street?"

Michael started to answer, but the older boy cut him off.

"How old are you?"

Michael blinked at the older boy.

"Look down there."

Instinctively, Michael looked in the direction the older boy was pointing.

John Joubert yanked the Exacto knife from his pocket

and slashed the boy's throat. He watched the skin fall away from the youngster's neck like the peel coming off an apple or tomato. If there was blood, Joubert didn't see it.

Michael Witham felt the steel slice across his throat. Then he saw blood spilling down his chest. He yelped, broke away from his assailant, stumbled, and almost lost his balance in the snow. Screaming, he ran down the hill and home clutching his throat, blood oozing between his gloved fingers.

Michael Witham's wound was two inches long and took twelve stitches to close. Again, the assailant had gotten away. Although all the attacks had occurred within a two mile radius of John Joubert's home on Cottage Street, no one in the neighborhood suspected him, and Joubert didn't think they ever would. Nor did he have any regrets about the things he had done. At least not until he returned from his uncle's house a few days later.

He'd ridden his bicycle the 130 miles to his uncle's home in Massachusetts; it took 13 hours for the return trip. But as tired as he was, he stopped off at his Scout meeting.

"Watch out for the Woodford Slasher," one of the older scouts counselled the younger ones as the meeting broke up.

Only then did John Joubert realize that his fantasies had caused real pain to real people, and that frightened him.

Or was he more afraid for himself? Afraid that next time he might not be so lucky. Afraid he might make a mistake and get caught. John Joubert decided that the attacks had to stop . . . at least for a while.

TEN

"I can't lie to you. I can't say I didn't do it, but the last time I plead guilty to anything I got the death penalty."

(John Joubert, February 6, 1988)

8:00 P.M., August 22, 1982

John Joubert's sabbatical from crime lasted two years, but his fantasies had continued to grow.

A few miles from downtown Portland was Back Cove, a popular attraction for joggers. You could find them out in force on good days—and the fanatics on cold and blustery days—trotting along the well-kept trails that wound through the countryside.

Ricky Stetson had jogged around Back Cove many times and had no reason to believe that he was in danger there. At eleven, red-headed, freckle-faced Ricky was small for his age—soaking wet he might weigh sixty pounds at best. Tonight he was wearing his favorite sweat suit; gray with raised red letters that spelled "U.S.A." across the front. Blue and white sneakers completed his outfit. He was headed up Marginal Way, a heavily traveled stretch of road, when the car pulled up beside him.

"Where you headed?" the man asked.

"Just jogging," Ricky Stetson told his father.

Ed Stetson, his wife Delores, and Ricky's sixteen-year-old brother Steve were on their way home. They, too, thought Ricky was safe. With an hour of daylight left and plenty of traffic around the Cove, why wouldn't the boy be safe? It was a two and a half mile run. Surely he'd be home by nine.

"See you later," Ricky said to his family as he jogged away from the car.

John Joubert had not wanted to join the Air Force; he believed that he'd had no other choice. Portland employers weren't exactly clamoring for the opportunity to hire a guy with little college education, and Joubert wasn't about to spend the rest of his life behind the counter at McDonald's.

Now eighteen, Joubert had left college after completing only ten credits during his first year. He'd had no choice about that, either, having fallen victim to the dreaded "Freshman Syndrome"; staying out too late at night and too far away from his books. Most of his time he spent in arcades playing video games. He'd often joked that his favorite class was "Asteroids 101."

But despite his grades, he'd enjoyed college. He'd taken his first alcoholic drink on Valentine's Day, had tried marijuana twice, and had become something of an expert on the game of "Dungeons and Dragons."

In Dungeons and Dragons, players assume the roles of mythical characters who are controlled by the Dungeon Master, or DM for short. More often than not, Joubert was the DM. Although in real life he still felt like an outcast, he more than compensated for this in his fantasy world. It took many hours to master the game, but the ultimate rise to power—deciding the course of events, deciding who would live and who would die—made it all worthwhile.

Those good times were over now. Even if the school would let him back in, he couldn't afford the tuition.

His mother had caught on to him, too; she'd made it clear that she expected him to start pulling his own share of the weight.

For relaxation, Joubert would ride his ten-speed out to Back Cove. He could forget his troubles up there, yet still have time to make it back for his nine o'clock curfew.

Just before nine o'clock, about halfway around Back Cove, Ricky Stetson's life ended. Six witnesses would later tell police that they'd seen him jogging on Baxter Boulevard. Each of them would describe him in detail, from his red hair down to his gray sweatsuit with U.S.A. printed on it in raised, red letters. All of them mentioned the young man following him, dark-haired, somewhere between fourteen and twenty years old, clean shaven, riding a ten-speed bike.

It had to have happened before nine; that was when the last witness had seen the Stetson boy. A few minutes later, a seventh witness saw the man on the ten-speed quickly peddling in the opposite direction while glancing back over his shoulder. This time there was no sign of the little red-haired boy.

At 7:06 A.M. the next morning, a passerby found Ricky Stetson's body beneath the pedestrian foot bridge across I-295. The boy lay on his side, right arm extended above the shoulder, his blood-streaked left hand resting on his stomach. Blood had soaked through his gray sweat top and dried to a rusty color. His pants had been tugged down halfway over his hips; a knot in the drawstring apparently had prevented the killer from pulling them all the way off. Because there were no puncture marks in Ricky Stetson's sweat shirt or T-shirt, and because dirt and grass had been found inside the shirts, Police concluded that the killer had had more success in removing those articles of clothing. Investigators from the Portland police department combed the water's edge for clues. They didn't find anything, at least nothing that would be of much help. They would never find the murder weapon.

One thing bothered lawmen. The boy had been stabbed in the chest, leaving a 3/4″ gash, but why the sharp cuts on his calf? The pathologist provided an answer: the child had been bitten—by his attacker. The pathologist had also determined, after studying the bite mark, that two of the killer's top row teeth were out of line.

The Stetson murder was to go unsolved for months. Eventually, police would make an arrest, but the man would be cleared in court, and the Stetson file would be thrown open again.

At the time of the Portland arrest, John Joubert was 1,500 miles away in San Antonio, Texas. Then, after completing basic training, the Air Force sent him to Biloxi, Mississippi, where he was just now beginning to get used to the life of an enlisted man.

Joubert hadn't attacked anyone since joining the service. Basic training had placed great demands on his time, and his lack of a car had greatly limited his mobility. But those weren't the only reasons; for the first time in his life, he'd built a solid friendship with a man his own age. They'd gone through basic training together and spent what little free time they had in each other's company. Joubert had always wanted a relationship like this, had always needed one. He shared much about himself with his new friend, but one secret he would never share. As Edgar Allan Poe had written in *The Man of the Crowd*, ''. . . some secrets do not permit themselves to be told. . . .''

ELEVEN

"From the second day I got there, I hated the place."

(John Joubert, on life in Nebraska)

Airman First Class John Joubert felt good about Nebraska. From his airplane window he watched the patchwork of corn and wheat fields slide by far below. The fields were so neatly laid out that Joubert could almost imagine some giant using a T-square and a table knife to carve up the land. Maybe Nebraska wasn't as pretty as Maine, but it would be all right.

The plane made a wide curve to the right and slowly began its descent to Eppley Airfield.

Joubert was in a good mood. He'd turned twenty a few days before. His best friend Erik Braden*—who had been with him since basic training and with whom he had a lot in common—had also been assigned to Offutt. And he was finally free. He'd finally escaped from the teasing, the rumors, the pain and suffering he had caused. All of it lay behind him, left in the dust of his backtrail.

A slight bump roused Joubert from his thoughts. The plane was on the ground, taxiing toward the terminal. Soon he would be on fresh soil.

It didn't take long, however, for John Joubert's en-

*Erik Braden is a fictitious name used for this person.

thusiasm for Nebraska to fade. For one thing, he could not get used to Nebraska's hot, humid weather.

"What's the matter, John?" Erik asked. "You look sick, man."

Joubert did not reply immediately. He was very pale, and his face looked pained. He stepped away from the car on which they were working.

"It's the heat, I think," Joubert said.

He went behind the garage and threw up.

John Joubert and Erik Braden were radar technicians, for which they received $100 a week, payable every third week. They'd gone through orientation together, had requested assignment to the same room and were put in barracks 400, room 113. The transition went smoothly at first, then things started to go wrong. Losing his lunch because of the heat had been only the first in a string of bad experiences.

About a month later, Joubert noticed that Erik had become distant, cold, speaking to him only in single words or clipped phrases.

"Erik, I know something's wrong. What is it?"

"Nothing," Erik would always say, as if it were a great inconvenience to say even that.

Joubert was not satisfied; he continued to press for a more suitable answer. Finally, Erik caved in.

"I'm getting another room."

"What? Why do you want another room?"

"I don't want to talk about it," Erik said tightly.

So Joubert began to snoop around, and soon he uncovered the reason his roommate wanted to leave.

Some of the other men had noticed that Erik and John were spending a lot of time together. Was it possible that they were not quite all man? Maybe even gay? The whispering rustled throughout the barracks like dry autumn leaves. Erik Braden would not stand for this kind of talk, and if it meant staying away from his best friend, well, that was the way it had to be.

Joubert thought of the rumors he'd hoped were buried with his past, and he burned with new anger.

"They think we're gay, don't they?"

"Yeah. Fucked up, ain't it?"

"Erik, we both know better."

Joubert wanted so much to reach out to his friend, to tell him it didn't matter what others thought, but nothing he could say would change Erik's mind.

"I've got to get another room," he said, his jaw set.

And that's what he did, leaving Joubert neither a roommate nor a best friend; the two rarely spoke during the month of August. One of the most important things in his life gone, Joubert fell into a deep depression.

He tried to fill his free time by working on his model planes. One day while in a lackadaisical frame of mind, his Exacto knife slipped and sliced his finger. Blood spurted out all over the table.

At the base hospital, a doctor stitched up Joubert's injured finger. The nurse gave him a roll of surgical tape, several packages of gauze for a dressing, and a box of thin plastic gloves to help him keep his dressing dry in the shower.

After the accident, Joubert looked for other ways to relieve his loneliness. One afternoon, he decided to offer his help to a local Boy Scout troop. He visited the Omaha Boy Scout headquarters where he was given the name of Donald Shipman, scout master of Troop 499 in Bellevue. Joubert called Shipman as soon as he got back to the base.

"Mr. Shipman, my name is John Joubert, and I understand you're looking for an assistant scout master. I'm an airman at Offutt, and I'd like to talk to you about the position."

Don Shipman had been a scout master for eight years.

He firmly believed that it was a scout master's duty to instill good values in the boys he worked with, and this young man seemed to embrace the same philosophy.

"Well, John, I really don't need any help right now, but when the boys get back in school we'll be starting up again. Call me then."

In late August, Joubert met with Shipman for the first time.

"I'm an Eagle Scout," Joubert told him, "and I've had experience helping with a troop back in Maine."

Don Shipman was looking for more than just an assistant; he wanted to find someone who could eventually take over the troop. Joubert's personality and clean-cut good looks immediately impressed the scout leader, who wanted just such a role model for his boys.

Shipman had a son about Joubert's age, and the interview went much like a father-son conversation. He could see no reason to question the young airman's sincerity, but he felt obligated to do a background check.

"I'll get back with you soon, John," Shipman said as he stood up to shake the young man's hand. "But let me say that I'm very impressed."

Joubert's supervisors all said the same thing:

"He's new here, but progressing like we think he should."

That was all Shipman needed to hear, so he called Joubert.

"Be here Sunday night the 18th," Shipman said. "I'd like to introduce you to the parents."

They did not get down to scouting business immediately; they talked about the disturbing news of the day: the disappearance of Danny Joe Eberle. Although most of the parents were concerned, they were not yet frightened. This discussion occupied the first half of the meeting, then Don Shipman suggested that they turn to other matters.

"Folks, I'd like to introduce you to John Joubert. He's an airman at Offutt and an Eagle Scout. He's originally from Portland, Maine, and he's our new assistant scout master."

They all were friendly, but other than that, the introduction caused no great stir. Joubert's name was even misspelled in the minutes. Afterwards, he shook hands with the parents and thanked them for welcoming him. Again, they discussed the missing paper boy among themselves, and Joubert listened with interest, his face showing all the emotion of a man trying to choose a tie to wear to the office. Joubert wondered what these parents would say if they knew that Danny Joe Eberle's killer was sitting here among them, among all their boys.

Why was it so easy, Joubert wondered, for him to listen to their talk and not be affected? Perhaps he couldn't believe that he had killed the boy. It seemed so unreal, like a dream, or like one of his fantasies. So he decided to make sure that it had actually happened.

Early the next morning, Joubert drove out to Base Lake Road. In the weeds not far off the gravel path lay the body of Danny Joe Eberle, stripped down to his underwear, hands and feet bound, just as Joubert had left him.

No, this wasn't a dream.

Joubert returned to the base and shut himself in his room where he masturbated, his victim's pleas once again ringing in his ears.

Bills were piling up, and Joubert's airman's salary couldn't cover them. In July he had bought a '79 Nova, a factory 4-speed with power steering, power brakes, am-fm cassette player, mag wheels and radials. He put $100 down on the car and managed to secure a loan for $2,988—which his father had to co-sign, giving his consent over the phone. But now Joubert felt the pressure of his financial obligation.

One night while out for a pizza, he noticed a sign on the counter:

DELIVERY MAN WANTED

Joubert was qualified for the job, and Domino's was willing to work around his nighttime schedule. He would have a regular salary, a bonus based on the number of pizzas he delivered, and he could keep the tips. He'd start work around four in the afternoon and quit when the job was done, and it would be done in ample time for him to get back to the base by 11 P.M. and begin his work there.

One day Joubert was playing a video game called "Time Pilot," in the same Kwik Shop from which he'd spotted Danny Joe Eberle, when a blond-haired boy walked in and took a position at the game beside him. The boy looked familiar. They made small talk for a few minutes while Joubert tried to remember where he'd seen that face. Finally, he gave up.

"Have we met before?"

"Yeah. I'm Jeremy Culver.* I'm in your scout troop."

A few days later, while on his route, Joubert spotted Jeremy, and again they talked. They found that they had a lot in common. Soon they became fast friends.

At scout meetings, Don Shipman noticed that Joubert had found a favorite, and that was just fine with him. The Culver boy needed someone to lean on, someone to talk guy talk with.

One afternoon, Jeremy invited Joubert home to meet his parents, and the airman noticed the Dungeons and

---

*Jeremy Culver is a fictitious name used for this person.

Dragons paraphernalia as soon as he walked into the boy's room.

"You play Dungeons and Dragons?"

"Sure do," Jeremy said. "I just started. You want to play?"

They would spend many hours playing this fantasy game that both had come to love. Again, Joubert took the role of Dungeon Master so he could control the game and the make-believe characters dreamed up by the younger boys who often joined them.

It delighted Don Shipman to see Joubert take such an active interest in the troop. Already well into middle age, Shipman had lately become more of a disciplinarian. The boys needed a younger man to play the good guy, to be one of them, and Joubert was making the most of that role. He even instructed them on safety precautions.

"Don't go with strangers," he told them, and after each meeting or outing, he made sure that every boy had a ride home.

Once, during a Scouting function, John Joubert met the mayor of Bellevue. After Don Shipman had introduced them, had told about Joubert's involvement with the troop, the mayor extended his hand.

"We need more young men like you," he said. "You're an asset to this community."

John Joubert beamed.

"Thank you, sir," he said, shaking the mayor's hand. "I'm glad to be here."

TWELVE

The Waldens were no strangers to Omaha, but neither were they thrilled about coming back to the city. Steve Walden, an Air Force meteorologist, had met his wife Sue there thirteen years before when both had been in the service. Sue had grown up in Syracuse, New York. Steve was a Missouri boy; with his blonde curly hair and boyish face, he looked something like Wayne Rogers. Their son Chris had been born in Omaha. Now the service had brought them back; Steve had been transferred to Offutt in July.

Like most parents after the Eberle murder, Steve and Sue kept a closer watch on their son. Chris had turned 12 only ten days after Danny Joe's death, and he knew better than to talk to strangers. Because they didn't have many friends, the Waldens had grown closer to their son during the summer, much closer than they had been just a year before.

A bright, freckle-faced youngster with a shock of sandy-brown hair, Chris had reached the age when only two things seemed to interest him: girls and video games. Unfortunately, his small allowance fell pitifully short of paying for his weekly video game fix, so he resorted to stealing.

His parents discovered this while stationed in Hawaii. After grocery shopping in the base commissary, Sue took out her wallet to pay and found it empty.

"That's funny . . ." she said, embarrassed, knowing she'd had money the night before. "I was sure. . . ."

This was not the first time cash had mysteriously vanished. Several weeks earlier, after hosting an Air Force wives dinner, she'd missed twenty dollars from her wallet. Immediately she suspected Chris.

"We've talked about stealing," Sue told him that night before he went to bed. "You know how your Dad and I are about honesty. Did you take that money?"

Chris put on his best poker face.

"I didn't take it, Mom," he assured her.

Sue wasn't convinced. A few weeks before, some friends had gone on vacation to Europe and left their son Philip with the Walden family. Philip's parents had given Sue two rolls of quarters for his lunch money. Slowly it dawned on her that Chris and Philip were playing more video games than usual at the snack bar down the road, and the more they played, the fewer quarters Philip had for lunch.

The clincher came a few days later when Chris couldn't eat any of the chicken dinner his mother had worked so hard to prepare.

"What's wrong, Chris?" Sue asked.

"I don't feel good."

"Come on, Son," his dad demanded. "What's the problem?"

"I think I had too many milkshakes," Chris said, after a hesitation.

"How many?"

"Five."

"Where'd you get the money?"

There was nothing for Chris to do but confess; he'd taken his parents' money and spent it on his friends. Chris's sudden confession almost made Sue laugh, but she fought down that urge. To learn that her son was stealing hurt her deeply.

"Today it's small change," she scolded. "Tomorrow it's hubcaps."

Convinced there was a problem, the Walden family went to a counselor to try to work it out. The experience seemed to bring them all closer together. At least the stealing had stopped.

Now back in Nebraska, they had little winter clothing and no friends. But they had one another and a chance to start over.

Again John Joubert was feeling his need to kill. The pressure had been building inside him these past few weeks, and he had to release it somehow. So once again, he went on the prowl for victims. After getting off work in the morning, he'd cruise the streets with his rope, tape, and his knife. But every time he spotted a potential victim, something happened.

One boy had stepped under a streetlight before Joubert could reach him. On another occasion the young girl he was stalking had turned a corner where there was too much traffic.

Joubert's young friend, Jeremy Culver, was confused about the Sarpy County killer.

"Why would someone want to hurt a little boy," Jeremy had asked more than once.

"He's a jerk," Joubert replied. "Just a jerk."

"I'm afraid. What if he comes after me?"

"Don't worry about it, Jeremy."

"I have these nightmares."

"Like I said, don't worry about it. It won't happen. I promise. . . ."

THIRTEEN

*"So many times we look back and say . . . if we
had only taken him to school that morning."*
(Sue Walden)

7:45 A.M., Friday, December 2, 1983

Sue Walden was in the kitchen fixing her son's favorite breakfast: peanut butter sandwiches and dry Sugar
Pops with milk on the side. She had long ago given up
asking why he ate the cereal and drank the milk sepa-
rately. She'd written it off as one of those pre-teen idi-
osyncrasies common to kids searching for their own
identities. Still, it made her laugh to think about those
Sugar Pops and the milk that would wind up together
anyway.

Chris came bouncing down the stairs in his brand
new tennis shoes.

"You can march right back up those stairs," Sue
Walden said, "and get on your winter shoes."

"But Mom," he complained, "I'm going to be late."

His mother was adamant.

"There's still snow on the ground. You'll get your
tennis shoes wet and have to wear them the rest of the
day."

"I have gym early this morning. It'll be all right."

"Now, Chris," she said sternly, giving him an I'M NOT KIDDING look.

Chris frowned, turned around, and stomped up the stairs, making sure his mother heard every step. Then his bedroom door slammed so hard that Sue could feel the vibration. After a few minutes, he came down again carrying his winter shoes.

"I'm going to be late," he said accusingly.

Chris ate his peanut butter sandwich in silence, then tugged on his coat for the eight block walk to Pawnee Elementary School.

"Don't forget your hat," Sue reminded him. "It's really cold out."

"It'll mess up my hair," he complained.

Sue smiled. Since Chris had been spending more and more time on the phone with young ladies, his appearance had become a top priority.

"I'm not worried about your hair. I'm worried about you catching cold."

She insisted that he wear the white stocking cap his grandmother had knitted for him. Grudgingly, Chris went to get the cap. He especially hated the small round ball of yarn on top. The boy picked up his backpack and, cap in hand, headed out the door.

Sue pulled back the curtains on the kitchen window. She could see her son fumbling with the cap as he moved up the sidewalk. Then, with a flip of his wrist, he tugged it over his head, flattening the hairdo on which he had worked for thirty minutes in front of the mirror.

Sue Walden didn't like to start off with an argument first thing in the morning, but at least she knew her son would keep warm and dry on his walk to school.

John Joubert pulled on his red plaid jacket and his Air Force–issue ski cap. Just after 6 A.M., he stepped out of the barracks. An icy gust hit him, and he shuddered. He'd heard on the radio that the wind chill was zero.

Joubert had the day off, so he went looking for victims. A young girl he'd spotted at a bus stop a few days before was not there this morning. He had counted on her being there. He looked around him; more people were out, traffic was picking up, and the day was growing lighter. If he didn't find someone soon, it would be too late to do anything today. He decided to try a different area. The neighborhood of Pawnee Elementary seemed as good a place as any, and it was nearby.

Eleven-year-old Mike Gooden was walking to school at about 8:30 when he saw his friend walking about a block ahead of him.

"Chris!" Mike yelled. "Chris Walden!"

Chris didn't stop; the wind had muffled Mike's shout. Mike called again, louder. Chris seemed not to hear, so Mike began running down the hill. The deep snow made it almost impossible to run, so Mike stopped trying to catch up. He decided to try calling one last time:

"Chris Walden!"

No response. Chris topped the hill and disappeared from sight.

John Joubert had been sitting in his Nova—parked at the side of the road, engine running, headlights on— for fewer than five minutes when he spotted the boy. He got out of the car and crossed the street.

"Hey, wait a minute," Joubert called.

Chris stopped and looked behind him.

"Can you give me directions?"

Like Danny Joe Eberle, Chris Walden believed in helping others; he waited for the stranger. Soon Joubert and Chris stood face to face. Joubert placed a hand on the boy's shoulder. With the other hand, he touched the sheath on his belt.

"Come with me, and you won't get hurt."

A bewildered, uncertain look crossed the boy's face.

Joubert's heart was thundering. Slowly he turned his head left, then right, checking for traffic.

A car came over the hill.

Instinctively, Joubert put his arm around Chris's shoulders, gently pulled on the boy, and the two of them began walking toward the Nova. They looked much like an older brother and a younger brother on their way to school.

As she drove past, Rebecca Trapani glanced at the older boy with his arm around the younger one, but she didn't stop until she reached the intersection. She checked the rear view mirror, studied them, and wondered briefly why she had an uneasy feeling about those two. When another car stopped behind her, she moved on.

"Get in the car and down on the floor," Joubert ordered.

The boy did as he was told. Another car went by, it's engine humming softly, and another woman glanced at them, but she didn't stop, either.

By the time Joubert pulled into traffic, Chris Walden was crying. He crouched on the floor to the right of his kidnapper, the tears flowing freely down his cheeks. Joubert felt sorry for him and even considered letting the boy go, but he came to his senses just in time. He couldn't release the boy now; he would surely go straight to the police. Besides, his need to kill was very strong now, and he'd been searching so long for another victim. No, he couldn't release the boy now; it was too late for that.

In the momentary confusion, Joubert had lost his bearings. He was now driving down an unfamiliar street, but he kept going straight ahead until he hit a road that he had heard of: Cornhusker Highway. He made a turn and headed for the dirt road and railroad tracks that he knew were nearby.

After about ten minutes, Joubert pulled to the side of the road and shut off the engine. The engine cricked as it cooled. Joubert got out of the car. The keys tinkled lightly as he shoved them into his pocket.

"Bring your books and come with me."

Head bowed, body trembling, Chris followed the man along the old railroad tracks that bordered a sparsely wooded tract of land. Then they left the tracks, and Joubert led the boy into a patch of trees.

"Do everything I tell you, and you won't get hurt."

Chris Walden stood shivering and crying. He did not know, nor did he care, that he was in a wooded area just off Giles Road. Nor did he know that he was only two miles from a television station that would soon be broadcasting news of his disappearance. He just wished that he were home.

"Take off your clothes," Joubert ordered.

Maybe if he did what his kidnapper wanted, Chris thought, he would be home soon.

Chris dropped his backpack and began to remove his clothing. First the parka. Then the shirt and pants. He stacked each article of clothing neatly on top of the backpack.

"Leave your underwear on," Joubert ordered as the boy was tugging off his socks. "Now lay down on your back."

Chris must have sensed something.

"No," he protested in a half-apologetic tone.

"I said lay down!"

"No!"

Despite the icy wind, Joubert was sweating. He placed his hands first on the boy's shoulders, then suddenly around his throat. Chris tried to pull away, but he wasn't strong enough. Gasping, he struggled frantically. Joubert tightened his grip and forced him to the ground. With the boy flat on his back, Joubert knelt on his chest and continued to squeeze as if he were wringing out a dishrag.

Chris Walden fought for his life. He squirmed feebly, pushed at Joubert, tugged at the hands that seemed like bands of steel around his throat. His face was distorted in pain and beet red. He couldn't breathe. His heart seemed as if it would explode. He tried to swallow, but that hurt almost as much as the fingers clamped around his windpipe. Chris began to shudder violently.

Summoning all of his energy, the boy tried to roll away, and he'd almost managed to break free when Joubert drew his knife and thrust it into Chris's back. Chris screeched. Again Joubert stabbed him. Chris continued to scream, but no one was near enough to hear . . . except the man who had caused the scream.

Several more times, the blade sliced through the air and made that sound of a spade hacking into damp earth. Chris Walden was limp, and he wasn't screaming anymore, but Joubert felt that he had to make sure the boy was dead. Without so much as a blink, he slit the boy's throat.

The white snow ran red with blood.

FOURTEEN

*"We knew he hadn't run away. We didn't know
that many people. Where would he have gone?"*
(Steve Walden)

4:30 P.M., Friday, December 2, 1983

Chris was late. It wasn't like him to be late. Soon it would be dark out. Where was the boy, anyway? Why didn't he at least call? Every few minutes, Sue Walden would look out the kitchen window, hoping to spot her son coming up the walk; each time she was disappointed.

Supper would just have to wait. Sue slipped on her own stocking cap and winter coat and went out into the late afternoon cold.

"Wait till I find him," she grumbled. "I'll ground him for a month for getting me this worried."

She could see him now, pressing up against some silly video game doing electronic battle with electronic aliens from an electronic planet. Surely he'd just lost track of time and was afraid to come home, afraid to face his mother's wrath.

Sue decided to retrace the eight block route that Chris normally walked to school. He had been kept after school before for one reason or another, and she hoped that this was one of those times. She parked the

108

car and went into the school building. The halls were deserted, deserted and still. Sue went straight to the office.

"Hi," she said to the secretary behind the desk. "I'm Sue Walden, and I'm looking for my son, Chris. I don't mind if he has to stay after school, but I need to know about it."

"Let me see if he's in one of the rooms," the woman said.

She got up and bustled out the door. Sue could hear the clicking of her heels fading down the hall.

Suddenly, Sue realized that she'd left both the garage door and the front door open, so she didn't wait for the secretary to return. On her way back to the car, she heard children laughing, then saw them sledding on a hillside a few hundred yards away. She scanned the group, trying to pick out her son's coat. In the fading light, she might not be able to recognize Chris at that distance, but she would certainly recognize his coat with the rainbow stripes.

Chris was not on that hillside, so she decided to stop at the home of one of Chris's friends. She couldn't remember the little boy's last name, but she knew where he lived. The boy was playing alone in his yard when she pulled into the drive. Sue got out of the car and approached him.

"Have you seen Chris?"

The boy looked puzzled.

"He wasn't in school today," he told her.

Sue's knees nearly buckled. Frantically, she dashed back to the car, yanked open the door, and slipped behind the wheel. She gunned the engine and roared out of the driveway and covered the four blocks to her own home over icy and snow-packed streets in less than a minute. Her husband, Steve, was getting out of his car when she slid to a stop at the curb.

"What's the matter?" he asked, staring.

"Chris wasn't in school today!"

For a moment, Steve did not move.

"Call the police," he said.

Sue rushed into the house and did just that. Then she decided to call his teacher, but she was shaking so badly and her eyes were so blurred that she couldn't read the names on the page of the phone book. Never in her life had Sue Walden been so terrified.

"Maybe they've made a mistake at school," Steve said. "Maybe he skipped his classes and is over at a friend's house."

Steve didn't sound convinced. He knew that this would be out of character for his son. Besides, it was dinner time. Not once did either Steve or Sue think of Danny Joe Eberle. All they knew was that it was dark, and it was cold.

Where was their little boy?

"No," Steve told the police officer, "he's never run away before. Where would he go? We haven't been in town long enough for him to make a lot of friends."

Suddenly overcome with emotion, Steve began to hyperventilate.

"My God," he said, gasping, "I hope I don't have a heart attack."

"Just take it easy, Mr. Walden," the police officer said. "We'll find your son."

Soon word got around that another young boy was missing. Seventy-nine days had passed since Danny Joe Eberle's disappearance, and the community had begun to relax. Now, only a few weeks before Christmas, a chill went through Bellevue residents, a chill that even the cold Nebraska wind couldn't match.

* * *

Sheriff Pat Thomas received the call on his car radio at the end of an exhausting day's work. Too far from the office, he decided to call John Evans from home.

Evans was attending a farewell dinner at Offutt Air Force Base for one of his best agents who would soon be leaving to start his new assignment in Chicago. Just as the first course was being served at the Officer's Club, Evans's pager started beeping. He frowned, dabbed at his mouth with a napkin, excused himself, and went in search of the nearest phone.

"We've got another one," Sheriff Thomas told him.

Evans hadn't expected this, and the news caught him off guard. He did not need a more detailed explanation; he knew precisely what "another one" was. But even this didn't overly concern him. Two or three children had been reported missing each week since the Eberle murder, and all of them had turned out to be runaways.

"How does it look, Pat?"

"It's a little boy who never made it to school. This one's for real, John."

Evans felt sick to his stomach. He'd been feeling sick a lot lately. A sickness brought on by anger, by fear, by dread. Just that morning the Eberle task force had been cut back because of fewer and fewer leads in the case. Now it had happened again.

John Evans hung up the phone. Then he walked quietly into the men's room and threw up.

F.B.I. agent Harry Trombitas was dispatched to the Walden home. He would stay with the family and await developments. A ransom call, maybe. Anything.

"If they want money, they've got the wrong kid," Sue told him.

"We need a picture of Chris for the ten o'clock news," Sheriff Thomas said. "As recent a photo as possible."

Sue knew exactly where to look. Some lovely class photos of Chris had been made just before they'd left Hawaii, but now she could not find them. A little panicked, she rifled through the desk drawers and came up empty, so she went through them again. The photos were gone. The wallets. The 5x7's. The 8x10's. All of them. Later she would learn that Chris had taken the pictures to school to hand out to his girl friends.

As she rummaged for the photographs, Sue could hear her husband thinking out loud in the other room.

"I won't even get mad at him . . . I just want him home."

The police finally had to settle for Chris's fifth grade picture. He'd gotten braces since the photo had been taken, but it would have to do.

All three television stations led off their newscasts with the story. Viewers were asked to closely examine the little boy's picture, and if they had any information that might help, to please call the Sheriff's Department.

In the Waldens' neighborhood, high above the housetops, a helicopter brought in from one of the local hospitals flapped through the night. The helicopter's search light cut a broad yellow swath across the snowy ground. Steve and Sue could hear the blades chopping, chopping, seeming first to fill the universe then fade away, then grow louder again as the helicopter circled back.

By midnight, Steve and Sue's hopes were dying. Chris's picture had been broadcast throughout the area, and still no word. Search teams had come up empty.

"I'd like you to go on television," Sheriff Thomas said, "and ask whoever has Chris to let him go. It might help." Then after a hesitation: "Of course, you don't have to do this. It's up to you."

Sue Walden had never been on television, and she didn't feel up to it now, but she knew what she had to do. The media was told that the parents would make a statement at 10:00 A.M. the next morning.

FIFTEEN

"Death is dreadful, but in the first springtime of youth, to be snatched forcibly from the banquet to which the individual has but just sat down is peculiarly appalling."

(Sir Walter Scott)

9:30 A.M., Saturday, December 3, 1983

John Evans picked up the Waldens at 9:30. As they drove downtown to the Sarpy County Sheriff's office, Steve was still trying to decide what he would say to the reporters. Sue gazed out the window at people she didn't know, searching in ditches and drainpipes and alleys for a little boy they had never met.

"Maybe he fell down and broke a leg or something," Steve said. "Maybe he's cold, but he's all right."

Evans agreed. There was no need to upset the parents until they were sure.

The news conference was held in a courtroom at the Sarpy County Courthouse. The Waldens sat between Agent Evans on the right and Sheriff Pat Thomas on the left. They tried not to fidget.

"Just make your statement," Thomas advised. "Don't answer any questions."

Steve wore a striped blue and green pullover shirt, his wife a royal blue sweater. He seemed like a shy little boy himself, a little boy who had wandered away from his mother. Sue sat with her hands at her side and did not speak. Although she never looked up from the table, the reporters could see the hurt in her face.

Then it was time to begin.

"Our son has been missing since 8:20 yesterday morning," Steve Walden said, his voice breaking at times, his delivery charged with emotion, eyes darting from side to side. "And we're very concerned about his whereabouts. If someone does have him, we'd like to have him returned. . . ." His voice now failing him, he added a tearful ". . . please."

Silence in the room.

Not one reporter tried to ask a question. They all seemed to understand, to sympathize.

The Waldens stood, turned, and left the room by the door through which they had come.

Lieutenant Jim Sanderson arrived home just before 4:00 A.M. He made a cup of coffee and carried it into the living room. The change in temperature was remarkable. It was at least ten degrees cooler in here than in the kitchen, but Sanderson didn't care. He'd been spending a lot of time out in the cold lately. He sat down on the sectional couch and leaned forward, both hands wrapped around a warm cup, and stared down into the black coffee. Steam rising from the cup warmed his face, and the coffee smell revived him a little.

Sanderson hadn't had a good night's sleep in three months. Ever since the Eberle murder, he'd been operating like a human computer. Cramming so much data into his brain, trying to retain as much as he could, trying to fit the little pieces together and solve the equation. Now his memory banks were threatening to overload. He was sure the killer had struck again.

Have I missed something? he thought. *Something*

John Joubert, Eagle Scout, January 27th 1981

Danny Joe Eberle

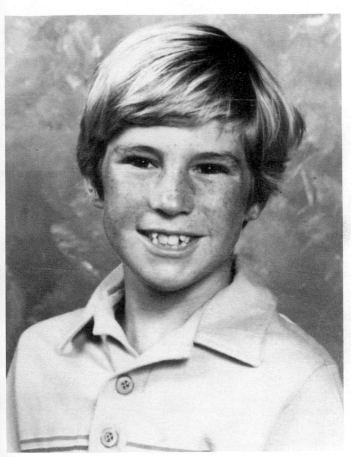

Chris Walden

Law enforcement officials gather at the site where Danny Eberle's body was found, September 21, 1983

Aerial photo of the site of where Danny Eberle's body
was found.

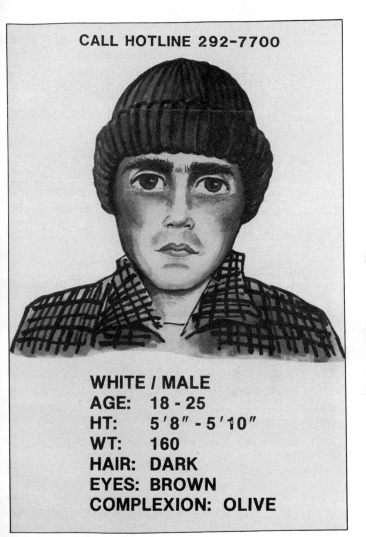

Artist's composite drawing of the suspect
in the Eberle/Walden case

Bob Ressler, FBI Agent, Psychological Profiles

Sarpy County Sheriff Pat Thomas

SARPY COUNTY
SHERIFF OFFICE
PAPILLION NEB.

'84

Bellevue Police Chief Warren Robinson

Lieutenant
Jim Sanderson of
the Sarpy County
Sheriff's Dept.

Joubert's car

Tape found in Joubert's car

Knife found in Joubert's car

A sample of Joubert's rope analyzed by the FBI, showing the colored strands

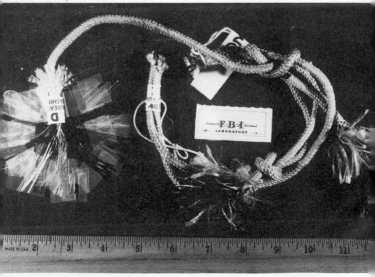

John Joubert, led to court hearing

John Joubert in prison, March 1987,
photo by John Haxby, KMTV

critical? Something so obvious that we could have solved this thing ages ago?

Then Jim Sanderson began to question his own ability as a lawman.

Why am I in charge? Why not someone else? There are others with more experience. Maybe the Walden boy wouldn't be missing if someone else were in charge.

Upstairs, his wife and daughter lay sleeping. Safe. Warm. It chilled him to think that somewhere another boy might be lying dead.

The Walden family lived only two blocks away. Two blocks. It could have happened to any family in the neighborhood. It could have happened to Sabrina, his own daughter. He didn't know what he would do if it were Sabrina. Long ago, Jim Sanderson had learned to hide his emotions, but now he was beginning to lose control.

As he sipped his coffee, which was already growing cold, a vision of Danny Joe's face swam into his mind, and suddenly he felt very close to the Eberle family. Danny Joe had been kidnapped in Sanderson's old neighborhood, across the street from his old home, in fact. He and Danny Joe had gone to the same junior high school. They even resembled each other with their "all American boy" look, muddy-blond hair, and dusting of freckles. He clenched his teeth and felt more like a failure than ever. He could also feel the pressure, the emotion, building deep inside him, threatening to erupt like a volcano.

The coffee and the strong emotions were upsetting his stomach. Sanderson set his cup on the coffee table and studied it in the dim light. It was very cold in the room.

First the sick feeling in the center of his chest spread to his limbs. Then his eyes began to burn. Then the tears came. Slowly at first, then faster and faster. They rolled down his cheeks and clung to the corners of his mouth, and he tasted salt, and they hung for a heartbeat at the edge of his jaw before dropping off into space. Sanderson had not cried like this in years. For a good hour he sat alone in the darkness, crying silently, feeling pain for the families of Danny Joe Eberle and Chris Walden. There was no shoulder for him to lean on. No shoulder big enough.

At least one hundred officers working on the task force, and they couldn't find one man. Certainly that man had killed again. Why wouldn't he? Who was going to stop him? Not Jim Sanderson, that's for sure.

Finally, exhausted, no more tears left to cry, Sanderson left the ice cold coffee on the table. Quietly he trudged up the stairs to his daughter's room. It was much warmer at the top of the stairs than it had been in the living room.

Through the open door, he could see that the clown face night light was doing its job, casting its pale light across the crib. His five-month-old daughter lay quietly on her side, eyes closed. She looked so perfect, so comfortable, so worry free. Everything she needed, he would provide. He and Terilyn.

Jim Sanderson suddenly became aware that he was smiling. Slowly, the smile wilted. How precious Danny Joe Eberle and Chris Walden must have been to their families. He tiptoed to the crib, eased himself down on the carpet, and for the next half hour sat cross-legged and watched little Sabrina sleep. He wanted to pick her up, hold her close to him, and never let her go.

What kind of world are we living in, he thought, *when a man's child can't live without fear?*

The long cry and this quiet time had done Sanderson good. Trying not to make a sound, Sanderson got up from the floor. He was a little stiff from sitting cross-legged for so long. On his way out, he paused in the doorway for one more look at his little girl. Then he went down to the kitchen where he made another cup of coffee.

According to the wall clock, it was now 5:40 A.M. He glanced out the window; the sky was already growing light beyond the distant hills. Members of the task force would be gathering soon, waiting for him.

Jim Sanderson breathed a tired sigh. Another night without sleep, and the nightmare it seemed was just beginning.

SIXTEEN

*"He [Joubert] was able simply to have no feel-
ings, to really not be able to identify with his
victims. He felt no sympathy, no sense of suffering. He was able to remove himself, as if they
were biology experiments."*

(Dr. David Kentsmith, psychiatrist)

3.00 P.M., Monday, December 5, 1983

Another day of miserable weather, miserable enough
to keep twenty-four-year-old John Szolek and his buddy,
Rodney Strong, off their jobs as concrete pourers. This
time of year, they averaged about two days a week at
work; much of the remaining time they spent out in the
field hunting pheasants and rabbits. So John wasn't surprised to get a phone call that afternoon.

"Hey, John," Rodney said, "let's go shoot us some
birds."

The temperature had not climbed above freezing all
day, and a frigid wind blew steadily out of the north,
occasionally gusting, sometimes driving a mixture of
fine sleet and snow ahead of it. Certainly not the perfect
day for hunting, but John Szolek wasn't about to let his
buddy down. They had been friends since junior high.
Just last year he had been a groomsman in Strong's
wedding.

"I'm on my way," he said.

They met at Strong's apartment and climbed into his burnt orange '75 Chevy pickup. The four wheel drive would have no trouble navigating the ice-covered streets that led to their favorite hunting ground: the fields near 108th and Giles Road. Strong, a bearded man of twenty-five, loved that place. He always seemed to find plenty of game scurrying about the fields and the woods. He'd been there last night and had killed four rabbits in less than an hour.

Strong and Szolek spent ten to fifteen minutes walking the first field. The blowing snow provided a perfect cover for the hunters as they scanned the landscape for signs of movement. Strong shivered. His new Levi denim jacket with the sheepskin lining was only a half-effective barrier against the icy wind. Szolek's favorite coat, an army green jacket, did a slightly better job. Both men wore their work boots, crusty bits of cement still clinging to the soles.

In his right hand, down by his side and pointed at the ground, Strong carried his .16 gauge shotgun. Szolek carried the .12 gauge Remington he'd had since he was a boy. Both weapons were single shot because any pheasant hunter knows that if two men can't down a bird with one shot, they have no business being out in the first place.

"Might be a little cold for the birds," Strong said, rubbing his hands together.

"It's just a matter of time," Szolek said, "Let's try a little farther west."

They returned to the pickup. Strong let it idle a minute to warm up. Then he drove to the spot where the railroad tracks crossed 108th Street. This was where he had killed the four rabbits; maybe it would prove lucky again.

The area around Giles Road is a perfect example of

just how close Omaha is to the country. Here, the road is dirt and gravel. You'll find open fields, long grasses, and some trees. Drive just a couple miles north, however, and you'll run into a business district and a busy intersection. But the Giles Road area is just far enough from the city to be considered "getting away."

No sooner had Strong pulled off the road than two rabbits shot past a few yards ahead of his front bumper.

"All right!" Strong said. "Let's get to it."

Strong was out of the truck before Szolek could catch his breath. Szolek grabbed his gun and jumped out, too. He watched his friend lope across the frozen ground and disappear into the brush. Then he heard the shotgun blast, a dull thud somewhat muffled in the falling snow.

"I got him!" Strong yelled.

Szolek moved deeper among the trees. Another blast, barely audible. Szolek waited, listening. Only the hissing of the wind through the trees.

As soon as Rodney Strong pulled the trigger, he realized that he had broken the law. Maybe it had been the low visibility, maybe the excitement, but for whatever reason, he had fired at a hen pheasant. Now the bird lay twitching feebly in the fresh snow. His hunter handbook stated plainly that hen pheasants were not to be hunted.

It was nothing compared to the crime that lay ten feet from the bird. His skin tingling, Strong gripped his gun more tightly, wheeled around and ran, crashing through the brush.

"Come on," he yelled to Szolek, "let's get out of here. We've got to get out of here."

"Rod, what's wrong, man? What happened back there? Did you kill that rabbit?"

"You don't want to see it, man. Come on . . . let's just go."

Szolek was not about to leave before he learned what had scared his friend. He followed his friend's footprints into the brush, Strong tagging reluctantly behind. Twenty yards deep, thirty, then forty. . . .

"Oh, my God!" Szolek yelled.

He stood staring down at the young boy clad only in a pair of white undershorts. The red splotches in the snow sent a sharp chill through his body. Instantly, he made the connection. He and his family had followed the accounts of the little boy who had vanished three days before. He'd watched the parents plead on the evening news for their son's return. Szolek felt as if his chest had been hollowed out; all he could think about was his ten-year-old brother Mike.

"What do we do?" Strong demanded. "My God, what do we do?"

By now, the importance of their discovery had begun to sink in, and they didn't talk at all during the drive back to Strong's apartment.

One glimpse of her husband's face told Kim Strong that something was terribly wrong. He had always been a tough guy, strong, secure. Now he was visibly shaken.

"What happened, Rod?"

"Find the newspaper. Just find the newspaper."

Goose bumps were beginning to crawl over her skin.

"What's going on, John?"

"It's terrible," Szolek muttered. He tried to elaborate but couldn't find the words. "Terrible."

Kim found the Omaha *World Herald* on the floor near the couch. The newspaper's pages crackled softly as she passed it to her husband. John Szolek stepped to Strong's side so he could see.

A picture on the front page. A picture of a smiling, freckle-faced little boy, his blond hair parted and swept roughly to the right.

"It's him," Strong breathed. "It's him."

Kim was confused at first, but as she listened, understanding came.

"What do we do now?" Szolek asked.

"We've got to call the cops," Strong said.

Szolek picked up the telephone receiver and dialed the number of the only policeman he knew: Ray Newbaurer of the Lavista Police Department.

Three rings, then a click.

"Ray? It's John Szolek. You gotta get over here right away."

"I'm just eating dinner, John," Newbaurer replied. "What's the problem?"

Szolek paused, then went on.

"It has to do with the little boy that's missing."

"I'm on my way," Newbaurer told him.

Sergeant Charlie Venditte stared out the cruiser window at the blowing snow. It had been his first full day on the Eberle/Walden task force. He'd been tapped to lead the assistance team from the Omaha Police Department and had been following up leads in Bellevue. Venditte was finished for the day now, and a Sarpy County sheriff's deputy was giving him a ride back to the station.

"If we don't find him soon," Venditte said, "we'll have a tough time finding him at all."

They were only two miles from the station when the radio crackled:

"Squad needed at 108th and Giles road. Body found."

Both officers had the same sick feeling; instinctively, they knew that their search had ended. The deputy turned around and headed west on the interstate. Within ten minutes they had arrived at the scene where a number of investigators had already gathered. Venditte recognized one of them as F.B.I. Agent Chuck Kempf.

"Hi, Chuck," Venditte said. "I'm Sergeant Venditte,

Omaha Police. I'm assigned to handle the crime scene for our department." Then, without waiting for an acknowledgment: "Is it Christopher?"

Agent Kempf didn't say anything, but the look on his face told Venditte all he needed to know. In his ten years as a police officer, he had seen that look many times.

The four men gathered around Kempf as he quickly explained how the crime scene would be handled.

"We've found footprints going in, and we need to preserve them. So please follow in each other's steps as we go in."

They all nodded in agreement and trudged in single file into the thicket.

The north wind made a lonesome swishing sound through the skeletal tree branches. It penetrated Charlie Venditte's overcoat and sent icy barbs through his suit and into his body, making him shiver uncontrollably. The snow was getting deep now. It crunched underfoot and quickly filled his leather shoes and melted, soaking his socks. His toes were going numb from the cold, but he tried to ignore the pain as he plodded through the night, following silently in the tracks of the officer ahead of him.

About forty yards into the brush they found the body.

My God, Charlie Venditte thought as he stared at the little boy in the snow. *Here it is Christmas time, a happy time. And look at this.*

Thoughts of his own family flitted through his mind. A few days before, he and his wife Mary had stayed up late putting together a bicycle for their four-year-old son. It had been a labor of love. They'd laughed and sung Christmas carols which still rang in his head:

Silent night, holy night.
All is calm, all is bright,

round yon virgin, mother and child.
Holy infant so tender and mild.
Sleep in heavenly peace . . .

The sight of the new snow stained with blood sobered him, shattering thoughts of his family and his son's bicycle. None of the officers spoke, but all were asking the same question: why?

A State Patrol investigator started snapping pictures. Charlie Venditte thumbed on his cassette recorder, and as the camera clicked and flashed, he spoke softly into the microphone. . . .

"It appears the victim has sustained what appears to be two unknown type puncture wounds to the back with blood dripping in a vertical position from the wounds. . . ."

As Venditte continued his description, the others sealed the crime scene. The boy's clothing lay scattered a few feet from the body. Slowly, an officer gathered it together: brown pants, red gloves, blue shirt—size twelve with red and white trim—and the brown shoes that his mother had made him wear to keep his tennis shoes dry. Inside the blue backpack, they found those tennis shoes along with a Star Wars "Return of the Jedi" notebook with CHRIS written across the cover.

Inside the right front pocket of Chris's pants, investigators found two shiny dimes. Twenty cents. Money the boy had planned to use at lunch for extra milk.

SEVENTEEN

"Almost every day after Joubert was arrested, I would ride by the jail, thinking how easy it would be to talk a guard into letting me into the cell with him [Joubert]. All I wanted was a leaded broomstick and five minutes."

(Steve Walden)

"We've got to get to them before they hear it on the news," Sheriff Thomas said, staring hard at the dark pavement flashing through the headlights and disappearing beneath the wheels of the car. "God, they can't hear this on the news."

John Evans nodded. Before this case, he'd never had to tell any parents that their child was dead. Not once in all his years with the F.B.I. Now he was about to do it for the second time in three months. He felt that sick feeling starting in his stomach again.

Sue Walden was in the kitchen when the doorbell rang, but before she could answer it, Sheriff Thomas and Agent Evans stepped inside. She stopped, wondering why they were here before 6:30, when the Waldens usually received the nightly briefing. Thomas looked her in the eyes, and somehow she knew what he would say.

"I'm afraid we've got some bad news."

Without speaking, Sue walked softly in from the kitchen.

"We've just found Chris's body," Thomas finished in a low voice.

Suddenly Sue screamed and dropped to her knees.

"Oh, my God . . . why . . . my God, why!"

The lawmen were not prepared for this reaction.

Thomas shuddered. When he was ten years old growing up in Falls City, Nebraska, a neighbor, an elderly Indian man, had passed away. For two straight days and two straight nights his widow had filled the neighborhood with her crying, moaning, and lamenting. Thomas and the other children had been afraid to go near the house. At that time in his life, he'd been mystified and frightened of death, and displays of grief made him uneasy. Now Sue Walden's screams had brought the experience rushing back vividly into his mind.

Steve Walden had been right behind his wife. Now he was at her side, trying to control his own grief so that he could comfort her.

"We're doing everything we can to find this man," Evans said, his eyes glistening with tears. "I promise you we'll get him."

Before they left, Thomas motioned for Steve to join him just outside the door.

"There's no doubt in our mind, Steve, but if you want, you can come down to the morgue to identify the body."

Steve Walden drew a breath of clean cold air and shivered. Then he sighed, his breath swirling like frosty cigar smoke in the stray light filtering through the window.

"No," he said. "I just can't do it."

Thomas nodded. Thomas and Evans went down the steps to their car and drove away.

The investigators worked through the night, doing their best to ignore the arctic-like weather. Every possible scrap of evidence had to be collected, logged, and sent to the lab. Special Agent Bob Ressler was summoned from Washington to put together another psychological profile.

The task force leaders met in the conference room the next morning to discuss the carving that the killer had made on Chris Walden's chest.

"It looks like some kind of leaf," Thomas said. "Who knows, it might be a marijuana leaf. Let's run down all the Hell's Angels again."

"Could it be the insignia from a Boy Scout badge?" Chuck Kempf said. "You know, their symbol?"

"You might have something there," John Evans said. "But how do we know it's a design?"

Kempf shrugged.

"This guy may just be so damn crazy," Evans continued, "that he doesn't know what he's doing with that knife."

Evans was happy now that the task force had been beefed back up to full strength.

"The key word here," Evans told his investigators, "is pressure. I want to pressure this community till it shakes."

Thomas knew that they were racing against time. They had to find the killer soon or the community might panic. The last thing he wanted were people taking up arms.

Once more young Jeremy Culver was questioning the actions of the Sarpy County Killer. Again he questioned his friend John Joubert.

"I don't know why those boys couldn't get away," he said, his face covered with an innocent look of disbelief. "I have some rope in my room," he told Joubert, "why don't you tie my hands behind my back and I'll see if I could get away."

Joubert was shocked by the idea and pretended not

to hear. "Come on John," the boy pressed, "I'm a Boy Scout . . . I bet I could get untied."

This time Joubert was forced to respond.

"I don't think so Jeremy . . . let's do something else."

"No John," the boy came back, "I have to know what it was like."

The irony of the suggestion brought a vision of Danny Joe Eberle shooting into Joubert's mind. Vividly he could see the boy's hands tightly bound with rope, the child struggling to get away. As quickly as it came, the vision was gone.

Before Joubert could answer, Jeremy Culver stood before him holding a strand of rope.

"This is silly Jeremy."

"Come on John, just do it."

Without another word Jeremy Culver lowered himself to the floor, his small hands reaching up behind him, begging to be bound.

For a second Joubert felt the rope in his hands, ran his fingers across the rugged strands tightly inter-twined. He didn't want to tie up his young friend but felt he had to . . . after all the boy was curious, but more importantly worried about his own safety.

Slowly Joubert slipped to his knees, gently wrapping the nylon rope around the boy's hands.

"Tighter," Jeremy demanded. "It had to be tighter."

Joubert did as he was told.

The Airman did not understand the feeling that soon overcame him. He began to enjoy what was happening, the feel of the rope against the child's skin.

Soon the rope was securely around Jeremy's hands and Joubert stood and backed away.

For the next few minutes he watched the child squirm on the floor. Frustrated, Jeremy Culver twitched and grunted as he tried with no success to free his hands.

For a moment Joubert lost his head. The feeble actions of the little boy were beginning to excite him. The scene was arousing his darkest side, quickly starting to outweigh his friendship with the child.

Again, Joubert could see Danny Joe Eberle struggling in the ditch just off Base Lake Road, then came the vision of Chris Walden's face wretched in fear as his attacker forced him to the icy ground. John Joubert's "need to kill" was again alive and lusting for more.

NO! STOP!

Suddenly something snapped in Joubert's mind, bringing him to his senses.

"NO! STOP!" he shouted at the boy.

Jeremy Culver was instantly still on the floor, his hands still no closer to freedom.

Joubert was quickly down on the floor to free the boy.

"That's enough," he scolded, "I told you it was a silly idea, I told you you didn't have to worry."

"Don't try that again," he warned, "you might hurt yourself."

NEVER AGAIN, Joubert thought to himself, *NEVER* get in the position again.

He had long ago promised himself he wouldn't hurt anyone he knew. In a few brief minutes however, he had come close to breaking that promise with one of the people he knew best.

NEVER AGAIN.

EIGHTEEN

"The anger and hate are gone now. We don't want revenge, what we want is for him [Joubert] to go to sleep and never wake up."

(Steve Walden)

This time there were witnesses.

Cheryl Baumgartner could not have been in a better mood. As she backed down the driveway, she glanced at the digital clock on her Celebrity's dashboard: 8:33 A.M., right on time. Cheryl was a cashier at the local Baker's supermarket. She had only one more day before starting her vacation, time she planned to spend doing her shopping and baking for the holidays.

The morning was clear and cold, and Cheryl could hear the wind moaning in the distance. Occasionally, a sudden gust buffeted the car, making it rock slightly. The roads glistened with a thin glaze of ice, so she was careful to brake slowly and to not make any sudden turns.

The intersection of Bernadette and 48th was a four-way stop. According to the yellow sign this was a school crossing zone, so Cheryl was not surprised to see the beige car pulled off to the side of the road in the lane just across the street. It was probably a father who had given his son a lift to school. She found it strange, however, to see the driver's door wide open.

"Shut the door," Cheryl said to herself. "It's cold out."

The two people in the other car sat with their heads together near the middle of the front seat. It seemed to Cheryl that they were arguing.

Lover's spat, she thought.

Or maybe it was a disagreement between father and son.

Then the intersection was clear, and Cheryl's thoughts turned from the beige car and its occupants to anticipation for her upcoming vacation.

"What a bummer," John Baumgartner said to his wife later that night.

They were on their way home from the early show at the Cinema Theater in Omaha where *Terms of Endearment* was playing.

"What do people see in Debra Winger anyway?"

"It wasn't the best movie I've ever seen," Cheryl said, "but I thought Debra Winger did a good job."

"She's not really good looking, and she's not a very good actress. I don't see what all the fuss is about."

Three hundred people had packed the theater that night to see *Terms of Endearment*, portions of which had been filmed in Nebraska. They'd come partly to see the movie and partly to see Miss Winger, who had caused a statewide stir when word spread of her romantic involvement with Governor Bob Kerrey. To many, it was almost like having a movie star as First Lady.

All of this made little difference to John, however. He would have rather been in the auditorium down the hall watching *The Right Stuff*.

"I still say it wasn't that bad," Cheryl said. "Besides, you get to pick the next movie."

"I wonder what's going on?" John Baumgartner said suddenly, his eyes fixed straight ahead.

"What?"

Then she heard the helicopter and after a few seconds picked it out far ahead of them, hovering close to the ground, its spotlight sweeping over the snow.

"It looks like they're looking for something," she said. "Or someone. . . . "

John Baumgartner was in his pajamas when Cheryl walked into their bedroom. He had the television turned to Channel 7. Cheryl sat down beside him on the bed.

". . . Chris Walden was last seen this morning," Carol Schrader reported, "between eight and ten. . . ."

Just then it clicked in Cheryl's head. She stared intensely at the television screen.

"John . . . I think I saw something this morning."

"What?"

"I saw two people struggling in a car. I thought it was a couple having an argument, but now I think I saw that little boy. What should we do?"

"Call the police," he said immediately.

"But it might not be anything. It would be awfully embarrassing if I'm wrong."

"You can't take the chance. You may have seen something."

Cheryl went downstairs to the phone in the kitchen and dialed 911. Within an hour, she was telling her story to police.

Cheryl was not the only witness. Rebecca Trapani had been on her way home from St. Bernadette's Church that morning where a friend's son had taken part in the services. As she was passing Pawnee Elementary School, she noticed an older boy walking with a younger one. Brothers, she'd thought at the time. Like Cheryl Baumgartner, she'd put the incident out of her mind until hearing about Chris Walden's disappearance on the evening news.

Both women wanted to be helpful, but they couldn't provide the kind of information the police needed.

"They don't believe me," Cheryl cried after the officers had gone. "I couldn't describe the car the way they wanted. I don't know a Ford from a Chevy. I told them everything I knew."

"You did the right thing," John said, trying to console her. "You did everything you could."

Cheryl still felt guilty. Why hadn't she realized the boy was in danger? Why hadn't she stopped to help? She could have at least stopped to see if anything was wrong.

Cheryl spent a restless night trying to answer these questions and others, trying to recall something, some little thing, that would help the police.

Please, Jesus, she prayed, before finally slipping into a troubled sleep, *help me remember.* . . .

NINETEEN

"As a result of the hypnosis, the plaintiff suffers from depression, change of personality, flashbacks and mental cruelty. As a result of these injuries, the plaintiff has been disabled and has lost the enjoyment of life."
(Rebecca Trapani v. the F.B.I. and Dr. Richard Garver, a lawsuit filed and lost in District Court, San Antonio, Texas.)

F.B.I. Headquarters, San Antonio, Texas
8:04 P.M., Tuesday, December 6, 1983

Rebecca Trapani sat fidgeting in the leather high-back chair, the kind of chair you might find in a banker's office or a judge's chambers. The seat was so high that her feet didn't reach the ground, but at the moment she was more concerned about what was going to happen to her. Occasionally, she would rub her right hand across her eyes and her forehead, then quickly return it to its grip on the arm of the big chair. She had heard about hypnosis but was skeptical. Even if there were the slightest chance that it might work, however, she was not eager to have them try it on her.

"Becky," said Special Agent Bill Kinney, who was an expert on hypnosis, "I'd like you to meet Dr. Richard Garver. He's been retained by the F.B.I., and we consider him to be one of the best at what he does. He's going to explain to you what's about to take place. When he's through, we'll ask you to sign the release form."

"Okay," Becky said.

"Mrs. Trapani," Dr. Garver said. "I want you to know that throughout this process you'll be in total control of your answers. If at any time your unconscious mind doesn't want to answer, it will let you know, and you please let me know."

"I'm not comfortable here. My feet aren't touching the floor."

An investigator left the room. In less than thirty seconds he was back with a shoe box that had "Gunslinger Boots" printed on the side. Dr. Garver placed the box under Mrs. Trapani's feet.

"How's that?"

"Much better," she said.

"Okay, Becky, I'd like you to look at the ceiling and try to focus on one certain area."

Becky tilted her head back, sought out a spot on the ceiling, and fixed her eyes upon it.

"Now, treat me as a boring speaker," Garver continued. "Just drift away . . . think of a warm fire burning in the fireplace, and concentrate on the flame. . . ."

Slowly he moved his hands toward Rebecca Trapani's eyes.

"Close your eyes and relax," he whispered. "Concentrate on that fire. . . . "

"I'm trying to visualize sitting in front of the fireplace," she told Garver, "but I'm having trouble seeing it."

"That's just fine. Let's try something different. Concentrate on a number, let's say 686. That's 6-8-6. Now, trying counting down from that number. Can you do that for me?"

"Yes."

"Okay, Becky, now I'm going to talk to your unconscious mind. I'm going to pinch your hand, and I want you to tell me as soon as you feel any sign of pain.'' Garver began picking at the skin on Rebecca Trapani's right hand. ''As soon as you feel the pain just raise your left hand. I don't want you to put up with any pain.''

Becky suddenly raised her left hand.

''That's it,'' Garver said. ''Now we're going to divide this hand into four different sections.''

He gently pulled the skin up from the back of her hand on the thumb side.

''This part will become rubbery and unfeeling. You won't be able to feel any sensation.''

Garver then dug his fingernail into her skin; the woman didn't flinch.

''This part of your hand,'' Garver said, touching the outside edge, the pinky side, ''will be very sensitive to the touch. Now I'm going to bring you out of the trance so we can talk further. Do you understand me?''

''Yes,'' Becky said.

''When you come out of this, I want you to clap your hands together three times, and you'll be able to recall everything I've told you.''

Rebecca Trapani opened her eyes and immediately clapped her hands three times.

''Now look at your right hand,'' Garver said. ''Remember I told you the inside part would become rubbery and insensitive? Take a look.''

''Oh, my!'' the woman said, ''you dug your fingernail in my skin.''

''And you didn't feel it, did you?'' Garver said, with a smile. ''That's how it works, Becky. I can talk to your unconscious mind, and you can still be in total control.''

''Yes,'' Becky said, offering a half-smile.

''Okay, Becky,'' Agent Kinney said. ''If you wish to

continue, we'll take a little time to read the release form and get your signature. Do you want to go on?''

"Yes," she said confidently. "I do."

It took less than five minutes to complete the necessary paperwork. First Becky signed the release form, then Agent Kinney, and finally Dr. Garver.

"All right, Dr. Garver," Kinney said. "Let's continue."

Garver moved closer to the woman.

"It'll be much easier to slip back into the trance now, Becky, and this time I'd like to tell you how to answer the questions I ask." Reaching for Mrs. Trapani's hand, he continued: "If I ask you a question, and the answer is no, simply raise the thumb on your right hand. If the answer is yes, indicate this by raising your right index finger. If your unconscious mind doesn't want to answer a question, raise these fingers. . . ." The doctor lifted the third and fourth fingers on her hand. "Do you understand?"

"Yes," Becky said, nodding.

"I'll be able to push you further into the trance by placing my hand on your shoulder like this. . . ."

The doctor touched his left hand to Becky's right upper arm.

"Let's go back now, Becky," the doctor whispered, "to last Friday morning. You told the officers you saw a man with a boy near the school, but you can't remember the name of the road. Even though you're not familiar with the street you know the route . . . try to remember. . . . You're in your car. Then can be now . . . now can be then. . . ."

"I can feel me there . . ." she said with a grimace, "but I can't see it. I can feel the frustration."

"Just take it easy and slow," the doctor said. "What about the car?"

"I can see part of the lights . . . but they won't come into focus. I feel like I don't want to be there."

No one said anything. The only sound was the soft hum of the video camera recording the session. Rebecca Trapani winced. She seemed to be going through some kind of inner struggle. A tear squeezed from between closed eyelids and tracked down her cheek.

"There's a part of me," she said, her voice cracking, faltering, "that's scared for the kid. I feel . . . I want to reach out . . . but I can't make myself do it. . . ."

"I don't want you to push," Garver said. "I don't want you to force. I'll help you. If you want to go deeper just ask me."

"I want to go deeper," she said immediately. "I want to go deeper."

Agent Kinney handed her a tissue.

"You have complete knowledge of what this individual looks like," Garver continued, touching Becky's upper arm. "You're in total control. Your unconscious mind knows what this man looks like."

Special Agent Kinney joined the questioning. Rebecca Trapani was their best lead, and he tried to take her back to the morning when she'd seen the dark-haired man and the boy near Pawnee Elementary.

"Are there more than two headlights on the car?"

A pause. Outside on the street below, a siren wailed. Becky's thumb moved: no.

"Are they round?"

This time her index finger: yes.

"Is the car a Ford?"

Yes.

"Is it a hatchback?"

No.

"What color is the car?"

"White," she said.

"Any hubcaps?"

Her thumb lifted: No.

"Any damage to the car? Any dents?"

No.

That answer, investigators would later find, was wrong.

"How about aerials, antennas?"

No.

"Decals?"

No.

Police would later find that this answer, too, was wrong.

"Were the windows up on the car?"

"Yes," Becky said. "The windows were up."

"Is the car a late model? Say, 1980 to '83?"

"Yes, it is."

"Have you ever seen this car before?"

"Yes, I have."

The investigators exchanged looks of surprise.

"Where? At a shopping center?"

"Yes."

"At a particular shopping center?"

"Southroads."

"Was it a week ago?"

"No."

"Was it two weeks?"

"Yes."

"Did you see the car in the morning hours?"

"No."

"Mid-afternoon?"

"Yes . . . it was down by Penney's . . . on a Monday . . . no, Tuesday. Yes, it was between one and two o'clock. About 1:30. I saw two people . . . a young boy with an older man."

"Is the individual white?"

"Yes, he is."

As the session moved into its second hour, Rebecca

Trapani seemed both physically and emotionally drained. She went on to give a detailed description of the man she'd seen for only a few seconds on the morning of December 2.

"I see a holster," she said, ". . . a gun . . . a knife . . . a holster . . . Carl's got one . . . he wears on his belt. It almost reminds me of a butcher knife. I've never seen a holster for a knife that long. . . . That man had his left hand on Chris's left shoulder like he was talking to him."

She saw the scene as clearly as she had that frigid morning in December. Suddenly overwhelmed by a sense of guilt, she began silently to cry again. Her tears seeped from behind closed eyelids and coursed down her cheeks. The hypnosis had brought everything rushing back, everything she could not possibly have remembered otherwise.

Why didn't I stop to help him? she asked herself. Maybe he'd be alive today if I'd stopped.

Agent Kinney gave her a tissue, and she dried her eyes. Then she was ready to continue.

"Finally, Becky," Kinney said, "is there anything significant we haven't talked about that you feel we should know?"

Her index finger twitched: yes.

"The look I was getting from the older male that morning . . . He was a phony . . . he was talking with the boy . . . yet he had this smile on his face . . . and at the same time he was glaring at me . . . that glare . . . he was trying to put on a smile, but he was just glaring at me."

"What kind of smile?"

"Like this."

The corners of Mrs. Trapani's mouth twitched, pulled up into a half smile, an ominous smile without warmth.

"If you were to see this individual again," Kinney asked, "do you think you could identify him?"

Her index finger jumped.

"Yes," she said immediately. "I do."

The interview had lasted two solid hours, but one question remained unanswered: what about the license plate number? Surely, if Becky were able to see the headlights, the taillights, and the holster on the man's side . . . why not the red numbers on the white background?

Five people had sat in the interview room, and not one of them had raised the question.

And Rebecca Trapani had missed an obvious clue that would have sent lawmen swarming through Offutt Air Force Base: the red, white, and blue decal in plain sight on the front left bumper of the killer's car. Without that sticker, John Joubert would not have been allowed to park on the base.

And without knowledge of that sticker, police had no reason to suspect that the man who had killed two little boys was spending the rest of his time serving his country.

TWENTY

"Dear God, please help me remember. . . ."
(Cheryl Baumgartner, writing in her diary)

F.B.I. Headquarters, San Antonio, Texas
Wednesday, December 7, 1983

Across the street at the Alamo a band was playing in commemoration of Pearl Harbor Day. At the moment they were in the middle of a Sousa march.

"Cheryl, we're sorry for the distraction," Agent Kinney said, "but we don't have air conditioning, and if we shut the windows it could get mighty warm in here."

Cheryl Baumgartner nodded. Unlike Rebecca Trapani, she felt totally at ease with Agent Kinney and with Dr. Garver. It took most of the first hour to explain the process of hypnosis to Cheryl. Then they put her into a deep trance.

"You're at the scene," Dr. Garver said quietly. "It's early morning. Just let it happen, Cheryl. Relax. . . ."

Then Kinney's voice, mechanical, monotonous. . . .

"The car across from you at the intersection. Is it yellow?"

A long pause. Then a flick of her thumb: No.

"Is the car white?"

Another long pause. The band across the street was

now playing *This Land is Your Land, This Land is My Land.*

Again the thumb: No.

Cheryl Baumgartner was not responding as quickly as the agents would have liked.

"I ask your unconscious mind to answer in a stronger manner," Kinney said. "Is the car in front of you a four door?"

No.

"Is it a two door?"

A forceful flick of the index finger: Yes.

The band finished its song, was quiet for a moment, then struck up *The Yellow Rose of Texas.*

"Are you aware of a license plate on the back of this car?"

No response. Cheryl seemed to be asleep.

"Is your unconscious mind aware of the presence of a license plate on the back of this car?"

Pause. Slight movement of her index finger.

"Is the license plate on the back of this car a Nebraska license plate?"

A movement of the two fingers next to Cheryl's pinky: I don't know.

"Is it an Iowa license plate?"

No response.

Agent Kinney repeated the question.

Cheryl sat in the high-back leather chair and did not move.

Finally, a slight movement of her thumb: Yes.

"Is your unconscious mind aware of the color of the license plate?"

Yes.

"Is the license plate background light in color?"

A short pause, then: Yes.

"Are the letters that appear on the license plate dark in color?"

Yes.

"Are the letters red?"

No.

A wrong answer, as investigators would later learn. Nebraska license plates that year had a white background with bold red letters and numbers.

"Are the letters on the license plate green?"

Yes.

"Does your unconscious mind know what the letters on the license plate are?"

Anchors Away was now beating through the window.

Yes, came the answer to Kinney's last question.

"Is the first figure on the license plate . . . is it a letter?"

No.

"Is it a number?"

Cheryl did not respond.

"Is it a figure or a letter?'

No.

"Is it a number?"

No.

"Are you able to vocalize the first thing you see on the plate?"

For the first time in over an hour, Cheryl spoke.

"It's a word," she said.

"Is it like a personalized license plate?"

"No. It's like commercial . . . or . . ."

"Like the word C-O-M-M? Let's ask your unconscious mind. Is the first word commercial?"

No.

"Is it some type of a word that has to do with some kind of special license plate?"

Yes.

"Does your unconscious mind know what this word is?"

Don't know.

"Focus your attention on the first grouping of letters or numbers that appear on the license plate. I suggest to your unconscious mind what I'm talking about are the numbers that are used to make the license plate unique. Does your unconscious mind have knowledge of what those letters or numbers are?"

Yes.

"Pertaining to those letters and numbers, is the first figure a letter?"

Almost imperceptibly, Cheryl Baumgartner's thumb rubbed the arm of her chair.

"I see a 'no' response," Kinney said. "Is the first figure a number?"

He was trying to narrow the field of search; in Nebraska, the first number on a license plate designates the county in which the vehicle is registered. The numbers are based on population and range from number 1 for Douglas County to number 93 for Hooker County.

"Does your unconscious mind know what that first number is?"

Yes.

"Is the first number a one?"

She did not respond immediately. Across the street, the band was well into *The Star Spangled Banner*.

Cheryl Baumgartner's index finger lifted: Yes.

"Is the second figure that appears on the plate a letter?"

No.

"Is the second figure a number?"

Yes.

"Is that number a one?"

No.

"Is that number a two?"

No.

"Three?"

No.

"Four?"

"*. . . and the home . . . of the . . . brave,*" the music wafted in through the window.

Cheryl's finger twitched.

"The first two elements of the license plate are one and four. Is that correct?"

No.

Kinney seemed frustrated by this apparent contradiction, but patiently he backtracked and began again.

"Is the first number a one?"

Yes.

"Is the second number a four?"

Yes.

"Is the third figure a letter?"

No.

"Is it a number?"

Yes.

"Number one?"

No.

"Two?"

No.

"Three?"

No response.

"Is it a three?"

Yes.

"Are the first three numbers associated with the plate 1-4-3?"

Yes.

"After the three is there another number?"

No answer.

"In the space right after the three is there another number?"

Yes.

"Is that number a one?"

No.

Again Kinney began the tedious process of trying to

identify the next number in the series. Finally, when he reached number eight, he got a positive response.

"The license plate your unconscious mind is reporting is 1-4-3-8. Is that correct so far?"

Kinney waited.

"I see no response. Are you able to verbalize?"

Cheryl sighed. Her head had been tilted to one side throughout the interview.

She'll have a stiff neck tomorrow, Kinney thought.

"I keep thinking about the word in front of it," Cheryl said.

"O.K. . . . But I don't want to concentrate on that word. The word might be commercial, disabled. It might be P.O.W., Medal of Honor, whatever—but I'm interested only in the numbers that make that plate unique. Are the numbers we have discussed so far correct? 1-4-3-8?"

Yes.

"Are there any other numbers? Is there a number after eight?"

Yes.

Again, Kinney started at one and counted up. When he reached nine, he got a positive response.

"Excuse me," Kinney called to one of the other investigators. "Could I have my pen back?"

Cheryl's index finger twitched upward, and she came out of the trance.

"I think I said yes to that," she said, and laughed, wiping her eyes with her left hand.

"I ask your unconscious mind to remember. 1-4-3-8-9. Is that correct?"

Yes.

"Is there another number?"

"Not too deep, Cheryl," Dr. Garver said. "Don't go too deep."

"After the nine," Kinney repeated, "is there another number?"

No.

"Is there a letter?"

No.

"Does your unconscious mind know what letters might be on the plate?"

Don't know.

"Do you see anything that makes this car different, a C.B. antenna, damage, rust?"

No.

"Are you aware of anything inside the car besides people?"

No.

"How about individuals inside the car? Is your unconscious mind aware of people in the car?"

Yes.

"Are there more than two?"

No.

"A male?"

Yes.

"Are you aware of how old he appears to be?"

Yes.

"Twenty to twenty-five?"

Yes.

"Is the individual a negro?"

No.

"Is he oriental?"

No.

"Is he white?"

Yes.

"Is he wearing a hat?"

Don't know.

"Can you see his hair?"

No.

"Does he have clothing on his upper body?"

Yes.

"A jacket?"

Yes.

"A solid color?"

Don't know.

"Is he wearing pants?"

Don't know.

"Shoes?"

Don't know.

"Have you seen this car before?"

Yes.

"Does your unconscious mind know where? Are you able to verbalize?"

As if on command, Cheryl snapped out of the trance.

"In the summertime, there was a car for sale on the lot. I keep thinking it's a county car, but I don't think that's right."

"Back to the license plate, Cheryl. Were the numbers green?"

Yes.

One of the investigators handed Kinney a booklet showing license plates from every state. He held it so Cheryl could see; slowly she leafed through the pages. Quickly she picked out plates from Colorado, then Florida.

"I know I'm saying yes to all of them . . . but I don't know why. I just keep seeing green. At first, I saw a word over here"—she moved her hand from left to right in front of her—"now I'm seeing a word up above."

"A word above the numbers?"

"What about a forester's plate?" she said impatiently.

Now two hours into the interview, Cheryl Baumgartner was becoming angry with herself. Agent Kinney could see that she'd had enough.

"I keep seeing a pine tree, but I can't tell if it's before or after the numbers. Do they have forester plates? I mean . . . I don't know what it is.''

"The time," he said, "is 12:44 on December 7th, 1983. At this time, we'll terminate the interview with Cheryl Lynn Baumgartner.''

Cheryl could not figure out why she was seeing the color green. The harder she thought, the more frustrated she became. So, when she returned to Nebraska, she drove back to the intersection where she'd unknowingly watched Chris Walden being kidnapped. Just off the sidewalk to the right of where the car had been parked was a small sign. A rectangular, green sign with a bicycle and a pine tree stenciled on it in white. BIKE ROUTE, the sign read.

The woman quietly sat in her car and cried. At least now Cheryl Baumgartner knew she wasn't crazy.

TWENTY-ONE

"No enemy can come so near that God isn't nearer."
(Sign outside a small church in Almer, Arkansas—a quote now carried in Barbara Weaver's wallet.)

If you were searching for the perfect All-American family, Warren and Barbara Weaver's would certainly be in the running. Deeply religious people, the Weavers believed the old saying: "a family that prays together stays together." They had a lovely home and were very close to their two children; everything that the All-American family might have except a white picket fence around their house.

Each morning, Barbara, a petite woman with graying dark hair, spent what she called "quiet time" with her children, Jason and Dana. It was a time for being together, a time for praying, a time to talk about problems and about dreams. Between September, 1983, and January, 1984, they devoted much quiet time to discussing the man who had killed Danny Joe Eberle and Chris Walden.

"Why would someone want to hurt children?" eight-year-old Dana asked her mother one morning.

"He's very sick," Barbara said. "Sometimes sick people can't help themselves."

"I wish I was big," said Jason, who was ten. "I'd be out there helping the police find him."

Barbara smiled at her son.

"Someday you'll make a great policeman," she said.

Quiet time always ended with the Weavers asking God to help the police find the killer. Jason and Dana—kneeling, small hands tucked beneath their chins, eyes closed, heads bowed—would take turns leading the prayer.

"Dear Lord," it would start each time, "thank you for this day. Please keep us safe at school and protect us from Satan. Please help the police catch the man who is killing these boys. Help him to be caught soon. In Jesus' name. Amen."

Then they would leave for school.

Barbara Weaver was the pre-school director at Aldersgate United Methodist Church, located in a quiet neighborhood just a few miles from her home. She enjoyed her work and was looking forward to the '84 school year because all of her budget requests had been approved, and she'd used the money to buy a language center for the children. Another reason Barbara liked her job so much was that her good friend, LaDonna Witschi, was her assistant.

On Tuesdays and Thursdays, Barbara and LaDonna worked with twenty-two, three-year-olds; the rest of the week they worked with children between the ages of four and five. Each morning began with a prayer followed by the pledge of allegiance. LaDonna admired the way her friend was able to inspire the children to learn.

On several occasions, while the children were involved in some task, Barbara and LaDonna talked about what they would do if the man who had killed Danny Joe Eberle and Chris Walden ever came to the school.

"I'd be very afraid," LaDonna confessed. "But I think this guy is long gone. Why would he stay around when he knows the police are after him?"

Barbara thought about this. Once, she had turned suddenly to find a man behind her. Her hand had jumped to her throat, and she'd let out a terrified shriek, perhaps startling Pastor David Kelly as much as he had startled her. Several times the pastor had managed to walk downstairs without them hearing him and had given them a fright. If only they could be sure that the killer had left town, then things would return to normal.

"I've always heard," Barbara said, "that if a person tries to rob you, give him anything he wants. But this man's a killer; if he comes here, it won't be to rob us. We have to protect the children."

LaDonna agreed, but neither woman knew exactly what they could do to make it safe for the children.

January 11, 1984.

John Joubert's car was in the shop, and he desperately needed cash, but that didn't bother him nearly as much as hearing Sheriff Pat Thomas refer to him as "a coward who could only kill children."

"If he were a real man," Thomas had said on television, "he would stop picking on children and start picking on someone his own size."

So Joubert decided to prove to Sheriff Thomas that he was not a coward.

Tuesday night it snowed three inches, but by the time Joubert got off work at six the next morning, the temperature had risen just enough to make the roads slushy. He went to the chow hall for a bite to eat, then back to his room for the rope, the tape, and the knife. He changed into civilian clothes, taking care to bundle up warmly for the trip. He went out and climbed into the Chevy Citation on loan from the dealer working on his Nova.

The car started right away.

Barbara Weaver, too, was up early, enjoying quiet

time. She had a lot on her mind as she sat down with her Bible scripture for the day. How lucky she and Warren were. They had two fine children and loved the community in which they lived. Then she thought about the pain that Judy Eberle and Sue Walden were suffering, and this brought tears to her eyes. She couldn't imagine what she would have done if Jason had been one of the murdered boys.

Dear Lord, she prayed, *I know I haven't given myself freely to you. I've been holding back. Please use me, Lord, in a special way today that I might do something to show your glory and your love. Amen.*

8:15 A.M.

John Joubert didn't know what he was looking for as he circled the neighborhood near Aldersgate Church. He'd slipped the knife up his sleeve where he could reach it in a hurry. The rope lay beside him on the seat. As he pulled into the pre-school driveway, he saw a woman sitting near the window inside the building. He circled the church once more than stopped on the gravelled drive. Joubert shut off the engine, which jiggled slightly, then was still. Silence. Except for the tick tick ticking of the cooling engine.

Barbara Weaver had seen the Citation pass the church twice. When the car turned in and pulled up to the door, she looked at its license plate: Number 59-L5154. Over and over again she repeated the numbers to herself.

The man opened the car door and stepped out, and Barbara Weaver got her first good look at him. The brisk breeze whipped loose strands of the man's hair about his head and fluttered the collar of his jacket. A chill started at the base of Barbara's spine and crept up her spinal column and spread through her body.

This was him. She knew it. She could feel it in her

gut. This was the man who had held her community hostage for 116 days.

The man stopped at the window and motioned for her to go to the door. Her heart was pounding furiously as she unlocked the metal door and opened it about three inches.

"Can you tell me how to get to 48th Street?" he asked in a quiet, slightly quivering voice.

Almost in tears, the man was trembling like a child who had wandered away from its mother. Barbara could not believe it. Calmly, she gave him directions, but she also burned an image of his face into her mind: about 5'5", brown hair, brownish green eyes, slight build. . . .

"Can I use your phone?"

The phone was just a few feet from the door; Barbara tried not to glance at it.

"There's no phone here," she lied.

Even as she said it, she realized how phoney it sounded. A pre-school without a phone? Suddenly, she felt very cold. If he thought she knew his identity . . .

Suddenly, he grabbed for the door.

"Get back inside or I'll kill you," he snapped in that same quivering voice.

Barbara Weaver acted on impulse.

She pulled the door open and bolted past the man and up the gravel drive. She had to make it to the road.

The cold wind battered the teacher's body, dried the tears on her cheeks. She slipped on a patch of packed snow. Her knuckles slammed into the pavement. Blood trickled from where the skin had been scraped away. Her hands were on fire, and her face burned from the wind. But the sound behind her made her forget the pain.

The sound of a car engine, of tires on the pavement.

He's trying to run me down! she thought.

Somehow she found the strength to struggle to her feet and continue fleeing down the hill toward the parsonage.

Nancy Kelly was in the kitchen when the front door crashed open, and Barbara almost fell into the living room. Mrs. Kelly rushed into the other room to see what had happened. Almost incoherent, Barbara Weaver was rattling off a series of numbers, repeating them over and over.

". . . 59-L5154 . . . 59-L5154 . . . 59-L5 . . . Call the police! 59-L. . . ."

Mrs. Kelly helped Barbara to a chair at the table.

"My God, Barbara! What happened?"

"It was him," she said, trying to gain control of herself, ". . . it was him and . . . and he tried to kill me."

Her face was wet and cold in the morning light.

"Now just calm down, Barbara. . . . It's all right now. You're safe. . . ."

Pastor David Kelly was upstairs preparing for his class on dealing with people under serious emotional distress. He glanced at his watch: 8:30 already. He only had a few minutes to make it to the hospital where the class was being taught. If he didn't hurry, he'd be late.

Suddenly he heard the commotion downstairs. He hurried down to the kitchen.

"Nancy. . . ."

Pastor Kelly froze in the doorway. Before him was Barbara Weaver as he'd never seen her before. Tear-streaked face, disheveled hair, slush-stained dress, bloodied knuckles. . . .

He'd always been impressed by Barbara's composure, but now she was anything but composed.

"Barb, what's going on . . . ?"

"He attacked me . . . the man who killed those boys."

"I've already called the sheriff," Mrs. Kelly said. "They're on the way."

It was now 8:40, and Pastor Kelly knew that the children would soon be arriving.

"I'll go to school," he said, "and tell the parents what's happened. Barb, you stay right here."

Pastor Kelly stepped out into the chilly morning just as a Sheriff's Department car pulled into the drive.

"She's inside. I'm going up to the school."

"I'll come with you," the deputy said.

Together, the two men walked up the hill toward the school.

On her way to the pre-school, LaDonna Witschi was driving a little faster than she should have been. Suddenly a Sheriff's car topped the hill. LaDonna automatically tapped the brake, but it was too late. She felt certain he'd pull her over. But the car whooshed past and turned into Pastor Kelly's driveway. LaDonna drove up to the pre-school, parked near the front door, and went inside.

The second she set foot inside, she sensed trouble. Barb Weaver's pocketbook lay in its usual spot on the counter, but where was Barb?

"Barb . . . ?"

Only the sound of the wind outside.

"Where are you?"

Silence. Somewhere, a faucet dripped.

"Barb . . . ?"

LaDonna was scared. She had hardly begun a systematic search of the room when she heard footsteps on the gravel outside, and this made her even more scared.

Then a soft rattling, a metallic clicking sound. The door opened. LaDonna closed her eyes, relieved, when Pastor Kelly and the deputy entered.

"There's been some trouble, LaDonna," Pastor Kelly said. "Get your coat and Barb's things."

"What's wrong?"

"I'm not sure," he said softly, "but I think Barb's been attacked."

Pastor Kelly's home was less than a block down the hill. They found Barbara there, still shaking, crying, in hysterics.

"Oh, Barb . . ." LaDonna immediately went to her friend and wrapped her arms around her. "What happened?"

"It was him," Barb said. "It was him. . . ."

9:15 A.M.

Barbara Weaver had been wrong about one thing: John Joubert had not tried to run her down with his car. He'd been as frightened as she, had just wanted to get out of there, get back to the base.

Now he was safe in his room. But how long would he be safe? He'd made a mistake, and he knew that when you started getting careless and making mistakes you ran the risk of being caught.

He was safe for now, however. No one could see him here in barracks 400, room 113. No one knew where he had been or what he had tried to do, and maybe he had gotten away quickly enough so that they would never know. He'd just have to be more careful next time.

John Joubert lay down on his bed to mull over these thoughts, and within a few minutes he was asleep.

TWENTY-TWO

*"I have a fear that he'll come after me some-
day . . . that he'll come after my children someday, to get back at me."*

(Barbara Weaver)

10:00 A.M., January 11, 1984

Lieutenant Jim Sanderson walked into the Bellevue
Police Department's conference room where several task
force investigators were discussing the case.

"I need someone to run out to Offutt Air Force Base
with me."

"What's up?" Chuck Kempf asked.

"An officer from Sarpy County just radioed in.
They've traced the car from an attempted assault at Aldersgate Church. It was a rental, but the guy has a
Nova, and he's from Offutt. Chuck, I think we should
go on this. I've got a feeling about this guy."

"Why?"

"I asked the dispatcher for the license of that Nova.
It was 59-R9397. Cheryl Baumgartner gave two of those
numbers under hypnosis."

Kempf knew that the investigation had been focusing
on the base lately. This just might be a lead.

"Let's go," he said.

Base security met Sanderson and Kempf at the gate.

"His name's John Joubert," the First Sergeant said. "He's over in Barracks 400. I'll show you where it is."

Thinking that the door might be locked, other officers from the Office of Security and Investigation (O.S.I.) had located Joubert's roommate.

Sanderson rapped on the door. They waited. Silence. Sanderson listened for movement but heard nothing.

"Open it," he said.

Joubert's roommate inserted his key into the lock, pushed. The door creaked as it glided open, but the dark-haired young man in the bed on the left side of the room did not wake up.

"Joubert!" the First Sergeant barked. "Wake up!"

Joubert opened his eyes. Still groggy, he frowned in confusion. At first he thought it was another inspection because his sergeant was there. But who were these other men?

"Get up and put on your clothes," the Sergeant said. "These men need to talk to you."

Chuck Kempf picked up Joubert's pants and shirt from the floor and tossed them to him.

"I'm Special Agent Chuck Kempf from the F.B.I.," he said, showing Joubert his identification. "And this is Lieutenant Jim Sanderson from the Sarpy County Sheriff's office. We'd like to talk to you about an attack at Aldersgate School."

"I don't know any Aldersgate School."

Joubert looked so baffled that Sanderson wondered briefly if he might be telling the truth. Much later, however, officers would learn that Joubert had thought Aldersgate had been a church. As far as he knew, he was telling the truth.

The O.S.I. agent pulled a card from his wallet and read Joubert his rights:

". . . you have the right to remain silent . . . should you give up that right, anything you say can and will be used against you in a court of law . . . you have the right to an attorney. . . ."

After he finished, the O.S.I. agent asked for permission to search the room. Joubert shrugged.

"Okay. Go ahead."

"Take him across the hall," Sanderson said.

Kempf and one of the O.S.I. agents led Joubert out. Sanderson and the other security officer began to search his room.

"I found a rope," one of the O.S.I. agents said a short time later.

He pulled it from a duffle bag and gave it to Sanderson. Sanderson's eyes widened.

"Jesus Christ. . . ." he said in disbelief. "This is the rope."

He handled it almost reverently, turning it over and over. He could not stop looking at the colored strands with which he'd become so familiar. Investigators had literally searched the world for the unusual rope.

2:00 P.M.

They took Joubert away in an unmarked car, his hands cuffed behind him. At the Bellevue Police Station, they pulled around in back and hustled him in the back door.

By now everyone on the task force knew who was coming through that door, and they looked up from their work as the officers and their prisoner passed. Many were disappointed. This man seemed so unlike the stereotypical killer. To instill such fear in a community, surely the man would have to be a monster, a big hulking brute, maybe with a scar running halfway across his face. They'd all waited anxiously for the monster, but a kid had walked through the door. A short, harmless-looking kid. Many could only shake their heads in disbelief.

Captain Don Carlson's office was tucked back in a corner of the main assembly room. The officers led Joubert into the office and told him to sit down on a chair in front of the desk. Through the open door, John Evans studied the prisoner.

Except for the eyes, Evans thought, *he looks just like the composite we circulated. He's so calm. So sure of himself.*

Evans had no doubt that the search had ended. He had waited a long time for this moment.

Suddenly, he thought of a movie that he'd seen not long ago on television. *Psycho.* Police had been questioning Norman Bates about a string of murders. With a quiet buzz, a fly had landed on his hand.

Bates had remained calm, trying to show investigators that he wouldn't even hurt a fly.

It's Norman Bates all over, Evans thought.

He shook his head and returned to the meeting with Sheriff Thomas and Chief Robinson.

"Let's have three men question him," Evans said. "One from each department."

Both Evans and Thomas would have loved to handle the job themselves, but they had faith in their men and thought that three could do a more thorough job than one.

"I want Sanderson in there," Thomas said. "Robbie?"

"Don Carlson," Chief Robinson said.

"And I'll send in Chuck Kempf," Evans said.

By now, Joubert's handcuffs had been removed. The officers—Sanderson, Carlson, and Kempf—led him down a hall, past a glass case displaying arm patches from police departments all over the country. During the walk to the south end of the station, Joubert kept his eyes on the floor.

They stopped before a door with a thin, brown plastic sign above it that said JUVENILE in big white letters. Carlson pushed the door open.

"In here."

The room wasn't very large, yet neither was it claustrophobic. Dark wooden paneling covered the walls. The low ceiling was made of some kind of white fiber material.

"Once again, John," Chuck Kempf said, "you have the right to remain silent. Do you understand?"

"Yes," Joubert said in his low, gravelly, New England accent.

They all sat at a long table. Joubert, sitting in an old swivel office chair, was nearest the door. To his left was Lieutenant Jim Sanderson, and to Sanderson's left, Captain Don Carlson. Chuck Kempf had taken the seat on Joubert's right.

"John," Carlson said, "first of all we'd like to talk to you about the assault on the school teacher. Where were you last night?"

"At work."

"At Offutt?"

"Yes."

"Why did you have the rental car?"

"Mine's in the shop."

"What were you doing at Aldersgate School this morning?"

Joubert sighed.

"I was desperate. I needed money for my car. I figured she had money."

"So you were out to rob her?"

Joubert nodded.

After a few more questions about his background and about the Barbara Weaver incident, the investigators took a break.

"Would you like something to drink?" Carlson asked.

Joubert nodded. Carlson stepped outside and asked an officer to bring a soft drink. Then the three interrogators huddled to discuss their next move.

"Show him the rope, Jim," Kempf said. "If he opens up, just take it from there."

Sanderson and Carlson returned to their seats; Kempf leaned against a metal desk. Again they advised Joubert of his rights.

"Are you aware of the Eberle and Walden homicides?" Sanderson asked softly.

A pause.

"I've read about them."

"Have you seen their pictures?"

Sanderson slipped the boys' school photographs from a large yellow envelope and laid them on the table. Joubert glanced at the photos.

"Yes."

"Let me show you something else, John."

Sanderson took the piece of rope from his pocket and offered it to Joubert for examination.

"One of the boys was tied up with rope. It's a rare piece of rope. We've looked all over the world for it, and we found pieces of it in your bag."

The color drained from Joubert's face, and they knew that this revelation had startled him.

"That rope's not rare," Joubert said. "I've seen it everywhere."

Sanderson explained that a special team had searched not only the country but other countries for the rope.

"We even went to Scotland Yard," he told Joubert. "Where did you get it?"

"From my Scout leader, Donald Shipman. We use it to tie knots."

For the next half hour, Joubert talked about his connection to the Scout Troop, then they took another break. The investigators had decided well in advance to build in plenty of rest time for the suspect. Everything had to be up front and on the record.

Chuck Kempf was extremely confident. He left the small room and headed for the main meeting room where he found his boss.

"There's no doubt," he told Evans. "This is the guy."

"How do you know?"

"He's very close. I think he's about to confess."

The questioning had been going on for several hours. It was dinnertime, and the order was placed. A Big Mac, fries, and Coke for Joubert. Three Italian sausage sandwiches for the officers questioning him.

"I can see it in his eyes," Sanderson told the others at their next private conference. "I think I'll try the split personality angle. I've got to give him an out."

Now it was just Sanderson and Joubert in the small room.

"You know, John, sometimes things happen that we can't control, you know. Maybe a 'Good John,' 'Bad John.' Maybe the bad John did this."

A very long pause. Then:

"Why don't you just tell me about it?" Sanderson said, leaning forward, touching Joubert's arm. He could see that the young man was on the verge of confessing. "Maybe the bad John killed them. Maybe he needs help."

Joubert began to rock back and forth in the swivel chair, his hands clasped together and clamped between his thighs, his lips quivering.

Is he going berserk? Sanderson wondered.

Sanderson got down on his knees beside Joubert and tried to calm him.

"Just take it easy, John. What is it?"

"Why did I kill those boys?" Joubert moaned.

The statement hit Sanderson like a thunderclap.

"It's okay, John. Now why don't you just tell me all about it?"

"I need to talk to Jeremy first. I've got to see him."

Sanderson got up and quietly left the room.

"See if Jeremy's parents will bring him down," he told an officer. "Joubert wants to talk to him."

A half hour later, Jeremy Culver was shown into the room.

"Hi, John," the boy said.

"Hello."

"Can I talk to him alone?" Joubert asked.

Chuck Kempf shook his head.

"One of us will have to stay here with you."

Joubert tried hard to think of a proper way to explain what was happening, but he could not find a way to express his feelings to his own satisfaction.

"Jeremy," he said finally, his voice almost a whisper, "I just want you to know that I'm involved in this, but whatever you hear, you were never in danger. I would have never hurt you."

The blond-haired boy stood silently and showed no emotion. He didn't want to believe what his friend was telling him. He wanted to believe that it was a dream from which he would soon awake. During the entire explanation, he looked deep into Joubert's eyes.

"Just remember what I told you," Joubert said.

Joubert and Jeremy embraced. It reminded Kempf of two brothers saying good-bye before the eldest left for college. Then Jeremy was led from the room.

"I'm ready," Joubert said.

Sanderson, Kempf, and Carlson brought their sausage sandwiches into the room and sat down in the chairs flanking Joubert. After so many hours of listening to the suspect, the room was beginning to seem very cramped and stuffy. Wearily, Joubert rubbed his eyes. Then, without prompting, he continued his story.

"I want to talk about the last one first, and the first one last."

None of the investigators objected.

"I picked up the Walden boy over by Pawnee Elementary. I guess it was around 8:30. . . . "

Captain Carlson took a pen from his shirt pocket and began taking notes. The pen made a soft scratching sound on the yellow pad.

"Are you writing all this down?" Joubert asked.

Carlson dropped the pen on the table. He did not pick it up again.

Sanderson listened intently to the details. Frustration was building up inside him again. He felt disgust and horror at the callousness of the crime, at the matter-of-fact way this man was recounting it. In his hand, Sanderson held a sharp number two pencil. Momentarily, Joubert's droning voice faded out, and the room blurred.

How easy it would be, Sanderson thought, *for me to take this pencil and ram it through his eye. . . .*

Then suddenly, the room snapped back into focus.

God, don't even think that, he scolded himself, feeling hot.

The sausage sandwiches, having lost their appeal, lay growing cold on the table; the men did not look at them again. They seemed almost obsessed with the story of the small man in the old office swivel chair. At one point the room was so quiet that the only sound besides Joubert's voice was a secretary's staccato typing in the next room. After a while it began to get on the captain's nerves. He tried to ignore it, but that only focused his attention on the noise. Soon the typing sounded to him as loud as the automatic rifle fire from the base range just a few miles away.

Captain Carlson got up, stepped through the back door, and whispered to the secretary:

"Stop typing. He's confessing."

The woman turned off the machine and left the room, and Carlson returned to his seat. The other interrogators hadn't even realized that he had left the room. They didn't have to encourage Joubert to talk; he was spilling his guts. Soon everyone in the station had heard the news.

TWENTY-THREE

*"I can never remember him showing up for any-
thing in four years of high school. He never
showed up for a dance, a football game, a bas-
ketball game, a party, anything. That's strange."*
(Thomas Balzano, a classmate of Joubert's)

10:00 A.M., January 11, 1984

A police cruiser was parked at the curb in front of
the Shipman home.

"What do you suppose is going on?" Don Shipman
said to his wife as he pulled into their drive.

Judy Shipman could not guess. Shipman got out of
the car and went to meet the policeman.

"Sir, are you Donald Shipman?"

"Yes, I am. What can I do for you?"

"I'm with the Bellevue Police Department, and we're
working on the Eberle/Walden murders. Do you know
John Joubert?"

"Yes," Shipman said, a little confused. "Why?"

"Sir, if we could step into the house, I'd like to ask
you some questions about him."

"That's fine with me, but what's the problem?"

They began walking toward the house.

"We have Joubert in custody for an attack on a school

teacher this morning, and we have reason to believe he's connected with the two homicides.''

''You've got to be kidding,'' Shipman said in disbelief.

Shipman opened the door, letting his wife and the officer go ahead of him into the house. The Shipmans sat on the sofa, and the officer in an easy chair across from them.

''Did you ever give him rope?''

''Sure I did. He was my assistant Scoutmaster, and he worked with the boys on tying knots. I gave him the entire training kit.''

''Then you'd be able to identify the rope?''

''Of course I would.''

''Would you mind coming down to the station with me to look at some photos?''

''Anything I can do to help,'' Shipman said.

While driving down to the station in his tan 1983 Honda Accord, Don Shipman tried to convince himself that this was a mistake. He would see the rope and know that it had not been among the pieces he'd given John Joubert for drills with the scouts. But when he arrived, and the officer showed him the F.B.I. photograph, he wasn't sure.

''Did you give John Joubert that piece of rope?'' the officer asked.

Shipman tried to remember. It frustrated him not to be able to remember.

''I probably did . . . but I'm not absolutely certain.''

Shipman knew that the rope must have been damning evidence or he wouldn't be sitting here holding this photograph in his hands. Still, he was not convinced that the police had the right man. One of his own sons had been stopped on the street and questioned about the case. Shipman had not been upset about that, nor was he upset now. The police were only doing their job; they had to talk to everyone who knew John Joubert.

"Mr. Shipman," the detective said, "we have reason to believe that Joubert may have kept the boys alive for some time before he killed them. He told us about some trailer that was often used for scouting trips. Do you know anything about that?"

Shipman nodded.

"It's the bed from an old Ford pickup. We all worked on it together. You know. Put a camper top on it so we could keep our scouting equipment in there. Surely you don't think . . ."

"Mr. Shipman, would you show us where that trailer is?"

Shipman hesitated only a second.

"Of course," he said.

Investigators waited until nightfall to move the old trailer. If it held any clues, the last thing they needed were a dozen or so reporters swarming around it.

Judy Shipman heard the Accord pull into the drive, and she met her husband at the door.

"What's going on, Don?"

"They've got John down at the police station," Don Shipman said reluctantly. He didn't want to tell his wife, but he felt she had to know. "They say he's the prime suspect in the murders of those boys."

Judy Shipman stared at him.

"But he's so quiet," she said. "So innocent looking. This just can't be."

Don Shipman didn't get to bed until well after midnight, and still he could not fall asleep. As far as he was concerned, the pieces just didn't fit. Suddenly, he sat bolt upright, causing the bed to jiggle, jarring Judy awake.

"Judy, there's no way in hell John killed those boys," he said. "Especially the first one. You remember? That was the night he was introduced to the parents. The meeting was held here, the same day Danny Joe Eberle disappeared. He was so calm and collected that night.''

''He sure was,'' Judy said.

She was trying to remember John Joubert's every move.

''And I talked with him not more than three hours after Chris Walden disappeared,'' Don said. ''I remember I was looking for him to tell him to change that weekend camping trip to a work day at the campsite, and I know for a fact he was with the troop all day that Saturday.''

The doubt was driving Don Shipman crazy. Abruptly, he flipped back the blankets and swung his legs off the bed. He snatched up the telephone receiver and dialed the Bellevue Police Department. Within a few seconds Sergeant Carlson had come on the line.

''There are some things I need to talk to you about,'' Shipman said. ''It's about John Joubert.''

''Come on down,'' Carlson said. ''I'll be waiting.''

Don Shipman got home a little after two A.M. He was tired and a little discouraged. He'd tried. He had done everything he could. He'd told Sergeant Carlson of how he was sure of Joubert's innocence. He'd told him how calm the young man had been at his home the day of Danny Joe Eberle's disappearance. He'd told about the weekend he had spent working with John, the same weekend that Chris Walden had disappeared.

''There's no way he could have held those boys,'' Don Shipman had said. ''I mean, we were in and out of his car all day, moving equipment here and there. . . . It just can't be him.''

Sgt. Carlson had listened patiently, as police officers were supposed to do. He'd nodded and had seemed to understand.

''Mr. Shipman,'' the Sergeant said, after Don Shipman had finished explaining, "we appreciate you coming forward with this information. Please, if you think of anything else, don't hesitate to call."

Shipman was not sure if the information had helped John any, but now a quiet peace had settled over his mind, and it didn't take him long to drift off to sleep. At least he had done everything he possibly could to help his young assistant.

TWENTY-FOUR

"If the state of Nebraska is bound and determined to execute me, what can I do? I'm not about to take my own life to cheat them."
(John Joubert)

The hearing was held in courtroom number two of the Sarpy County Courthouse on July 3rd, 1984, a day after John Joubert's twenty-first birthday. Most of the spectators could not take their eyes off the young man in the bright orange jailhouse coveralls.

Joubert didn't seem to care that he was being stared at. Nor did he seem to care when Deputy County Attorney Mike Wellman stood up at the table across the aisle to reveal for the first time what Joubert had told officers on the day of his arrest. Wellman was a small, pensive-looking man of thirty-six. With a forefinger, he nudged his wire-frame glasses so they rested more snugly on the bridge of his nose. Quickly, he scanned the papers in his hands, then began reading from the fifty-eight page confession. The courtroom was hushed as he read. Joubert appeared bored. At one point he propped his head on his right elbow and seemed not to be listening.

On several occasions during the two hour hearing, Judge Ronald Reagan interrupted to address the defendant:

"Mr. Joubert, do you understand what's happening here? Do you understand your rights?"

"Yes, Your Honor," Joubert answered each time.

One hour and forty minutes into the proceedings, Joubert and his attorney, Public Defender Jim Miller, were called to the bench to enter their plea. They had spent considerable time together trying to plan a defense, and together they had decided on the only course of action they felt would keep Joubert out of the electric chair: earlier in the day they had informed Judge Reagan that the defendant would be withdrawing his plea of not guilty. Now the Judge looked sternly down at Joubert and asked:

"How do you plead to the charges of first degree murder in the deaths of Danny Joe Eberle and Christopher Walden?"

Joubert did not speak right away. When the answer came, it was barely audible.

"Guilty."

"Mr. Joubert, you realize once you enter a plea of guilty it cannot be withdrawn."

"Yes, sir."

"What I'm telling you is that this is the final act."

Joubert nodded.

Judge Reagan jotted down a few words, sighed, looked back at Joubert.

"You are now adjudged guilty," he said, and set sentencing for October 9th.

A buzz of conversation swept the courtroom. Reporters hastily scribbled into notebooks. Some of them rushed out to find telephones. A few minutes later sheriff's deputies escorted John Joubert out the back door of the courtroom.

As allowed by law, Judge Reagan asked that two other jurists join him on a sentencing panel, and State Supreme Court Justice Norm Krivosha appointed Judges

Theodore Carlson and Robert Finn. Together they'd decide whether John Joubert would live or die. They would look at the good things about the man and weigh them against the brutality of his crimes. In legalese, this translated into "the mitigating and aggravating circumstances." To help them with this task, they studied the reports of three psychiatrists who had performed psychological examinations on Joubert. All the doctors agreed on one thing: John Joubert had known exactly what he was doing.

Dr. Bruce Gutnick, hired by the defense, concluded:

Diagnostic Impression:
  1. Obsessive Compulsive Neurosis, 300.30
  2. Sexual Sadism, 302.84
  3. Schizoid Personality Disorder, 301.20
Discussion: It should be clear from the above, that Mr. Joubert is a very sick and extremely complex individual. His primary form of satisfaction in life for 14 of his 20 years has been through bizarre fantasies followed by masturbation. The nature of these fantasies stems, in my opinion, from latent and unconscious homosexual desires which are unacceptable to his conscious mind, and from a confusion between sex and violence. For him there is no difference between sex and violence. Note that he uses the term, "cruising" to describe his search for victims, and his use of the term "pick someone up." These terms are commonly used by individuals who are seeking dates. Mr. Joubert is totally obsessed with his fantasies. This characteristic includes his obsession with details, such as his concern that he made parallel cuts, not star-shaped cuts in one of the victims. Note also that it was very important to him that he killed these boys "by the manual," meaning a step-by-step ritualistic method had been developed. It was further important

to him that he did these acts neatly, getting no blood on himself. These details all point to a ritualistic obsessive compulsive behavior pattern which was not fully in his control.

At this time he states that he consciously knows what he did was wrong. He is not sure that he could have stopped himself at the time, however. He is aware of the charges against him in detail, and is certainly able to participate in his own defense.

. . . Strictly speaking, in my opinion, Mr. Joubert was aware of his behaviors and may have been aware at the time of their wrongfulness. He was most definitely not psychotic at the time of his behaviors. However, his disorder results in compulsive behaviors which at points in time cannot be resisted by the conscious mind of the individual. That is to say, in my opinion, Mr. Joubert's actions were driven by unconscious forces which were outside of his conscious control. Once these unconscious drives gained control of his activities, I do not believe Mr. Joubert was able to stop himself.

Another report came from the Topeka Psychiatric Center:

Psychological tests reveal an I.Q. in the superior range of 123. He is well-organized, compulsive, and efficient.

He displays a remarkably emotional sameness, and discussed the homicides in the same way he discussed his work. His voice broke on one occasion and he became momentarily tearful when relating that the homicide scenes recur in his thoughts.

"I haven't been able to forget."

For the most part, however, there is an emotional coldness and aloofness. Although polite and imme-

diately responsive to questions, I felt no good rapport with him. He is separated in a remarkable way from his feelings and, in the same manner, is unable to grasp or understand the feelings of others. The psychologist came to the same conclusions: "He is totally out of touch with feelings. To protect himself, he remains isolated, withdrawn, and avoids intimate contact with people. There are also suggestions of a suspiciousness and lack of trust in people."

The patient denies awareness of any strong feelings of anger or any other emotion during the homicides. Afterward, he experienced regret that the deeds had been accomplished, but strictly in relationship to himself. He wondered how he could engage in such behavior; "it wasn't me." He made no comment about his victims, their experiences, their families.

He relates that, since age 7 or 8, he has wondered occasionally what it would feel like to kill someone. He says it was just an idle thought and that at no time did he fantasize how he might commit murder. In relation to the two homicides, he said, "I still haven't found out." When I reminded him that he had, indeed, killed, his response was, "But did I find out?"

Concerning the major legal question, the medical evidence suggests that the patient's behavior does not meet the legal test of insanity. He has a psychiatric disorder, and the homicides are attributable to irrational forces working on this man. In effect, it was "crazy" behavior, unexplainable by any sensible, definable motive. He appeared to be impelled by forces he could not control. At the same time, his cognitive intactness, good assessment of reality, preparation for the forays, and adequate assessment of what he did argue against his being in a state of not knowing right from wrong and not knowing what he was doing.

Diagnosis: Axis II—301.20 Schizoid personality disorder with compulsive features.
—Herbert C. Modlin, M.D.

By far the most stinging diagnosis came from Omaha psychiatrist David Kentsmith:

Mixed personality disorder with obsessive compulsive and schizoid traits.

Discussion: The behavior which has resulted in the murder of the two victims seems to be the culmination of a well rehearsed fantasy he played out during periods of solitude and self stimulation for the past 14 years and an inability to empathize. The fantasies continue even today. Apparently the fantasies have not been satisfying enough and he has sought to carry out the fantasies in reality. His psychological responses to the examination indicate he is an extremely bright, neat, meticulous and well organized person who works quite efficiently by the book following a routine. He seems completely isolated and separated from his emotions and has little or no ability to empathize or understand how others might feel. His attempts to provoke pain in others may be a way of trying to experience for himself some real emotion or feeling. His pursuit of his victims, the method in which he murders them is part of a very well rehearsed and clever game.

His pattern of behavior and the crimes he has committed are well known in forensic psychiatry. It is also known that the behavior is often associated with sexual arousal. Such persons are at high risk to repeat their crimes. Treatment methods have not been successful in allowing such individuals to control their impulses. There are several instances in which such individuals who were thought to have been success-

fully treated, once released from a secure and controlled setting resumed a pattern of murdering. Such individuals do experience at least intellectually a sense of remorse and superficial guilt. They cannot however identify with their victims or appreciate how it would feel to be subjected to what had happened to their victims. Psychiatric treatment in a secure hospital setting may help such persons develop more of an ability to appreciate the effects their acts have on others. The therapy however cannot be expected to change their basic personality structure or make them safe to be free in society.

There is nothing in this entire examination nor in the examinations of the three psychiatrists to indicate that Mr. Joubert was insane at the time of the crimes. He understood the nature and quality of his acts and the consequences of them. He also understood what he was doing was wrong and that he would deserve punishment. He had the ability to adhere to the right and his judgement was such he could choose to conform his behavior to the law.

He is competent to stand trial and has a superior ability to cooperate with his attorney in providing for his own defense. At the present time he is experiencing a degree of depression which is situational and associated with the suspense, isolation, and pressures surrounding his trial and upcoming sentencing. In general however, he finds a lot of satisfaction in the attention and focus on him which in some way allows him to feel important and of some value.

The three-judge panel had three months to make a tough decision. Even today they are not ready to talk about it. Should Joubert live or should he die?

TWENTY-FIVE

"He's a cold, ruthless killer who likes to kill little kids. If he gets out of prison, he'll kill little kids again. It's as simple as that."
        (Pat Thomas, Sarpy County Sheriff)

August 29, 1984

Sue Walden answered the phone on the third ring.
"Hi, Sue. It's Barb."

Immediately she recognized Barb Hamner's southern accent. After Chris's disappearance, Barb and several F.B.I. agents had all but moved into the Walden home so they could be on the spot if a ransom demand came. After they found Chris's body, the agents remained in case the killer called. During those months, Barb and Sue had become very close.

Sue was happy that she wouldn't have to return to Nebraska for the trial, a possibility she'd worried about all summer. It made her sick to think of being in the same room with the last person her son had seen. The Waldens hadn't even followed news coverage; they just wanted to forget.

"Sue," Barb said, "the judges will soon be sentencing Joubert. It's a three-judge panel, and I think it would be a good idea if you and Steve sent them a letter."

"What should we say to them?" she asked.

"Just get your two cents in, that's all. Tell them what Chris was like and that you want Joubert to pay for his crime."

"I feel like we should do it, and I think Steve would say yes. I'll talk it over with him tonight."

"It's just a suggestion, Sue. You do what you want, honey."

"Thanks again, Barb. Bye."

Two days passed before Sue Walden could force herself to sit down at the word processor in her husband's study. She didn't know what to write. How could she put Chris's whole life into a few paragraphs? So she sat for a long time, occasionally dabbing at her eyes with a tissue, staring at the blank monitor screen. When she finally put her fingers to the keyboard, the words came straight from her heart:

> *Dears Sirs:*
>
> *As I sit to write this letter, I am aware that this is probably the most important letter I shall ever write. I am writing in regard to the sentencing of John J. Joubert.*
>
> *I would first like to tell you a little bit about our son; our only child, Chris.*
>
> *We just moved to the Omaha area after four years stationed at Hickman AFB, Hawaii. Although we were reluctant to leave Hawaii, we looked forward to our assignment at Offutt. Chris was our own "Cornhusker" as he was born in Omaha, September 28, 1971. . . .*

. . . it had been a drawn out and painful process; Chris wasn't about to come into the world without a struggle. Sue had been in labor for more than eight hours. . . .

. . . Chris was what you would probably consider an average twelve-year-old, gaining a degree of independence, trying to etch his place with his parents, his teachers, and friends he made at school. He was a bright boy with an aptitude for computers, loved video games, and although his penmanship left a lot to be desired, he could draw cartoon characters with a flair. Chris took an interest in airplane models and was always building elaborate structures with Lego blocks. He wasn't crazy about vegetables, but couldn't get enough of pizza. . . .

Was she getting her message across? Or was she rambling? After reading this letter, would the judges understand how much Chris meant to her and Steve?

. . . Chris was a loving, trusting boy, trying hard to do the very best he could. We love him very much . . .

. . . she could not see the screen through her tears; quietly, she sat and wept until she was able to continue. . . .

It is ironic that Chris's life began in Omaha with such promise and joy and end [sic] so tragically in Omaha just a short twelve years, two months, and four days later.

He never had a chance.

We miss him terribly and when we think of all the things he will never be able to do we are filled with great sadness. . . .

. . . she was trembling so badly that she had to stop again until she could compose herself. . . .

Chris will never have a "first date," get a drivers license, graduate high school or attend college. Growing up is a happy time, sometimes painful, worrying about being "popular," getting acceptable grades, earning enough allowance to buy that heart's desire. As parents we try to teach our children the difference from right and wrong, good manners, and the Golden Rule so, hopefully, our children grow up to be responsible and caring adults—an asset to our society. . . .

. . . now her tears were angry tears, and she poured all of her anger and hurt and pain out through the word processor keys onto the screen. . . .

When we think of what Chris must have gone through on December 2, 1983, we feel guilty for not being able to protect him and shudder at how confused and scared he must have been. I keep thinking that if I had driven Chris to school that day he would be alive today. Although we don't know all the details of what happened that fateful day, we are convinced that Chris was at the wrong place at the wrong time. It could have been anybody's child. It is obvious to us that Mr. Joubert was waiting for the opportunity, having already thought out his plan. We are convinced that he had every intent to abduct a child and eventually, stab that child to death. Not just a chance meeting—a whim.

Mr. Joubert had already killed one young boy, and didn't get caught. He must have thought no one would ever guess at what he had done.

Mr. Joubert lived in the barracks at Offutt, in close proximity to his peers and apparently no one had a clue that Mr. Joubert was a murderer. He must have been terribly confident, with the lack of conscience to be worried about being found out. The very fact that he was able to work and behave "normally," looking at the composite of himself at his duty station, without any emotion, no remorse for ending the lives of Danny Joe and Chris is pretty difficult for us to deal with. . . .

. . . she was quaking with rage. She had the urge to scrawl across the page in big red letters: DON'T TAKE THIS LIGHTLY! OUR SON WAS AN INNOCENT VICTIM. HE NEVER DESERVED THIS.

Chris Walden's life ended December 2, 1983. It could have been one of the other children walking to school that day. The thought scares the hell out of us. Does Mr. Joubert deserve a life sentence? Is Mr. Joubert the kind of person that could be rehabilitated into our society? We think not. The bottom line here is: no matter what happens to Mr. Joubert, it will not bring our son back to us. Chris's death is something we will spend the rest of our lives trying to accept.

. . . before their son's murder, Sue and Steve Walden had been undecided about the death penalty. They'd discussed the morality aspect, had wondered if it were really a deterrent to murder. Now, although they were not happy about their decision, they had made up their minds. . . .

We seek justice here and implore you to exercise your authority for the death penalty for Mr. Joubert. We are in complete agreement concerning this matter and hope to God Mr. Joubert never, ever gets another chance to murder another child. We cannot stress this too strongly.

We are thankful we had the opportunity for some input on this case. If this letter is a little too long, it's because we find it difficult at best to express how we feel. Anger, frustration, fear and finally, despair at the loss of the person so very dear to us. We seek justice, not revenge. Please be certain Mr. Joubert will never commit murder again.
Respectfully,
Stephen C. Walden
Susan M. Walden,
Parents of Christopher Paul Walden

After more than six hours, she had finally finished the letter. It had been one of the most difficult tasks of her life, and she was emotionally exhausted. Her cheeks still wet from crying, she read over the words on the computer screen. Once, then twice, she checked for errors. Occasionally, her vision would blur, and she'd have to stop and blink away the tears, then search for her place and continue reading.

Satisfied that the letter said what she wanted it to say, Sue pressed the PRINT key. A couple of computer clicks, then the printer began buzzing, committing her words to paper.

When Steve Walden came through the kitchen doorway a few hours later, he knew immediately that his wife had been crying.

"What's wrong?"

"I've written the letter, Steve. It's upstairs."

He didn't say anything, turned, went upstairs to the study. The letter rustled softly as he picked it up from the desk, and read it. He could have written it himself, though not half as well. It was uncanny, the way Sue seemed to have read his mind, the way she'd captured the essence of Chris. He picked up a pen, changed a word here and there, fixed a grammatical error or two.

Then he signed it and the next morning sent it on its way by Overnight Express to prosecutor Mike Wellman.

The prosecutor had asked Judy Eberle to write a similar letter and, like Sue Walden, she felt that it was necessary. Also like Sue Walden, she didn't know what to say. And to make matters worse, her husband was against the idea.

"If you want to write a letter," Leonard Eberle said, "do it. I don't have anything else to say."

"Well, I do have something to say," she snapped.

Judy sat down with a pen and tablet at the dining room table. She stared helplessly at the blank page. Nearly a year had passed since Danny Joe's death, but the hurt was still as deep, still as cutting as ever. Finally words began to come. She had to force them out at first, then they came in a rush:

September 4, 1984
Dear Judge Reagan, Judge Finn, and Judge Carlson,
To introduce myself, I am Judy Eberle, Danny Joe's mother. Danny Joe, the young 13 year old boy, whose short life was spent helping people, friends and family and who in a short time gained many close friends because of being very firm in his beliefs of what was right and what was wrong and often standing up for those beliefs. For such a young person, he was wise beyond his years and loved and was loved by his family and friends greatly and we'll never forget him.

Then there's the Danny Joe that was snatched from life, very unsuspectingly and cruelly by a person that not only made Danny suffer, but made one more young boy suffer before he was stopped. Such a contrast and so unbelievable that this hearing is to decide whether this admitted killer of young boys will be allowed life or death. Why are we being so kind to a killer?

Joubert, admittedly, thought about letting each boy go before he killed them. Danny even asked if Joubert would take him to the hospital after Joubert had stabbed him. Danny promised not to tell who had stabbed him and if Joubert had known Danny he would have realized that Danny would never have told who stabbed him, as that was Danny's way.

Joubert never allowed his victims a, quote "choice of life or death," he just snuffed out two beautiful lives because he decided to.

I am making a plea to you three judges that Joubert be given the death sentence, which would be the same type of "choice" he gave my son and Christopher Walden.

There are so very many crimes against children and the crimes are increasing daily in number. Why do people feel they can interrupt such lives and instill such fear in children so a normal life isn't possible? I feel it's because the criminal doesn't have to face a death penalty if caught. The threat of death when someone interrupts a child's life, whether it be murder, kidnapping, pornography or etc. should be automatic. If strictly enforced, children will have more rights to be children and not suspicious young people never able to venture out and grow. Children of this age don't have the freedom I had as a child, the criminal has more protection than they do. Please think about this when you make your decision.

Thank you for your time.
Sincerely,
Judy Eberle

My husband feels I "said it all," so he won't be making a separate statement.

Judy didn't know if the letter would do any good, but she'd had to write it. She folded it carefully, tucked it into an envelope, licked the flap and sealed it. She wouldn't need a stamp; this was one letter that she would deliver personally.

September 11, 1984.

Beverly Joubert had been hit with too much, too fast. She still could not believe it. All those years while John was growing up she had not recognized his problem, had not picked up on the tiniest clue. But he was her son; whatever his crime, she could not let him die for it. So she decided to write a letter of her own:

Dear Honorable Judges:

As John's mother I feel compelled to write on his behalf. John's arrest was a great shock to me and to everyone who ever knew him. I still have a hard time believing this is all happening. It was an even greater shock to learn that my son has been mentally ill since he was six years old. Assuming the psychiatric reports are accurate, he has been bearing a great burden alone for many years. He has added to his burden the memory of killing two young boys. This will be with him forever.

Many people feel he is not remorseful for what he has done. I believe he is. His first words to me when I was allowed to talk to him on January 12th were, "Yes, I did it. I'm sorry." On other occasions he has told me he wished this hadn't happened and he wanted to be able to start over.

We all know this won't happen. John has been taught to accept responsibility for his own actions. He knows he can't blame anyone else for what happened. He is prepared to accept punishment.

As you know from John's psychiatric reports and Dr. Gutnik's testimony, John is a very intelligent person. If John is sentenced to death, that intelligence will be wasted. If John is allowed to serve a life sentence, that intelligence could perhaps be put to use to help other prisoners. John has always had good leadership capabilities. Why couldn't this be put to good use in prison.

John is not a bad person. Yes, he has caused a great deal of pain and suffering to many people, both here in Nebraska in the families and friends of the Eberles and Waldens, and in Maine and Massachusetts in his family and friends.

He is also suffering. Today I was allowed a contact visit with John, and I talked by phone with him for some time this evening. I know he's hurting and there's nothing I can do.

I can only depend on the Court's compassion and as a mother plead with you to consider the good in John.

This has been a very difficult letter for me to write because, again as a mother, I understand what the mothers of Danny Joe and Christopher have felt. When I first heard about John I felt as though he had died.

Thank you for taking the time to read and consider this letter.
Sincerely,
Beverly A. Joubert

. . . later, the sentencing panel would say that these letters "have provided a catharsis for those writing them . . . but have no probative value or weight in our determinations. . . ."

TWENTY-SIX

"It is a cruelty to the innocent not to punish the guilty."

(Unknown)

Tuesday, October 9, 1984

The decision was unanimous.

The three-judge panel found John Joubert's crimes went beyond brutal and heinous; they were "totally and senselessly bereft of any regard of human life." Because the panel felt that the aggravating circumstances far outweighed the mitigating ones, it sentenced John Joubert to die in the electric chair.

Now, years later, Joubert still sits on death row. One by one his appeals have been denied. The Nebraska Supreme Court has upheld his death sentence, and the U.S. Supreme Court has refused to hear the case. Still, by most estimates, Joubert is still years away from dying for his crimes.

Even death row hasn't stifled Joubert's need to kill. At twenty-five, fantasies of death and murder still rise to the surface from the darkest corners of his mind, but he claims to be in control of those thoughts. In fact, he expects someday to walk out of prison a free man. There are, of course, many people who want to make sure that day never comes.

In my conversations with the victims' families, I've come to realize that they no longer seek revenge for what he did. They seek only justice. Just as John Joubert carried out his brutal killings, so does the State of Nebraska now wait to carry out its legal "need to kill."

Many years from now, people will still be talking about what John Joubert did. Not only to Danny Joe Eberle, Chris Walden, and their families, but also about what he did to the community in which they lived. The fear instilled in so many by one man who in real life was meek and timid but in his fantasy world was a giant driven by a bizarre obsession with death.

Every now and then, Omaha police officer Bob Sklenar pulls out the yellow envelope he received a few days after John Joubert's arrest. It contains a letter from a ten-year-old girl. To Bob Sklenar, the words she wrote in pencil on the yellow paper make up for all the long hours he and the other officers had spent on the case:

Dear Bob,

Congradulations [sic] on your helping to find the killer who killed Danny Joe Eberlie [sic] and Christopher Walden!

Thanks bunches!

It takes a load of [sic] my mind. I've been having lots of nightmares about him killing me or my friends.

I sure hope there aren't any more people who are like him.

This man went to an all-boys school and got teased and beat up so he took it out on little kids.

Your friend,

Jennifer Walker

P.S. Thanks again and again.

P.P.S. You're my hero.

POSTSCRIPT

*Sorrow for the death of a father lasts six months;
sorrow for a mother, a year; sorrow for a wife,
until another wife; sorrow for a son, forever.*
                                    (Sanskrit)

Before 1983 they had been strangers, women who might
have passed unaware of each other in a supermarket. But
in tragedy, they became sisters. Each lost a son, one of
them her only child. The words you're about to read were
written by the mothers of Danny Joe Eberle and Chris
Walden. They are the words from shattered hearts, from
women who have had to face what the rest of us can only
pray will never happen to our families. Each wanted the
chance to send a "thank you" to those who supported
them through the crisis; each wanted others to learn from
what had happened to them. I haven't edited these letters
in any way; that was my promise to them. I thank them
for sharing their thoughts, and I respect them for their
courage.—Mark Pettit

A note from Judy Eberle:

*My friends know me as Judy. Strangers refer to me
as Danny Joe's mother. I was Danny Joe's mother,
but I am Judy. That's terribly sad for me, but Danny
Joe is in the past but for his soul and memories.*
  Danny's death started a long chain of events. This

in turn changed my attitude on life and caused an interest in psychology and spirituality. Also my values changed and I discovered friends to be the most important. Material things don't give "hugs" and say "I understand" when it's Danny's birthday or death date. Friends realize I will never be able to not hurt inside, time does not heal. Time only allows me to bring the hurt under control so that I can exist in the manner society dictates.

I discovered and am terribly sensitive to parents who don't realize how dear and precious their children are. Young children cannot be expected to adhere to adult or society standards as strictly as adults are able to. Love your children, truly love them, care for them, understand them and protect them. A lot of people are getting careless!

I discovered the love and support my community of Bellevue, Nebraska, and surrounding area offers. There's also a negative side to that I'm afraid. I discovered the lack of privacy after such an incident. Seems I am now "owned" by the community and can't reclaim my life again.

I discovered how quickly and efficiently the Bellevue Police and F.B.I. help a family. I have tremendous respect for them.

I discovered that a family that "prays together" doesn't necessarily "stay together." Each person tends to need their own space in order to deal with their own unique feelings. It caused our family to separate. This is very common and was necessary.

I discovered how to think "positive" and to draw the very best out of any situation. Nothing made sense until I did that for myself. It is still a real challenge to continue this type of thinking. But I must.

I discovered how to prevent other people's crude uncaring comments to become any part of me.

I discovered God is a large, loving, caring part of me. That "He" and I developed my spirituality, where religion is not a part of my life at this time.

Last but not least, I've discovered that when a person lives such a tragedy, that if you open, you learn tremendous things about life and spirituality that others are not able to accept or understand. But I consider it a true blessing when a person doesn't understand my thoughts on such. I know then they haven't had to go through what I have.
Thank You and Take Care,
Judy

A note from Sue Walden:

Well, you finished the book. How do you feel? What are you thinking? Are you asking yourself "do such things actually happen"? Could this happen in my neighborhood, in my community? To someone I know, to my child, to me? I can't really know what you're thinking or how you feel about what you've just read, but I can answer one of these questions. Yes, it happens.

Let me introduce myself. My name is Sue. I'm Chris Walden's mom. When we were interviewed by the author for the writing of this book, Mark asked us if we'd like to contribute a few words. I agreed. I was pretty apprehensive though, wondering what I'd say. It's kind of an amazing thing to me that someone actually wrote a book about a killer, two young boys in Omaha, Nebraska, and their untimely deaths, and one of those boys just happened to be your son.

I could spend hours telling you what it's like to go through something like that. How you can open the door to a time in your life and still experience the same confusion, the utter helplessness, the unrealistic quality and paralyzing terror that nightmares are made of. If you've ever lost a child somehow, by an illness or accident, you can relate to what I'm talking about. There's a definite sense of loss that is a real struggle to adjust to. I think it's harder to adjust to the loss and the knowledge of how Danny Joe and Chris died. Each to be snatched off the street and terrorized in ways we'll never know about and come to the end of their lives, each with multiple stab wounds, to be found days later in some obscure field. Unbelievable.

I'm probably never going to read this book. There may be some details of what happened during the time Chris was with his killer that we're better off not knowing. What difference could it possibly make? My reason for wanting to write a few words here though is not to tell you my side of the story, but to let you know that even when things get really tough, there are always people around, ready, willing, and able to help you out.

It would be difficult and unrealistic for me to think I could thank everyone who was there for us December 2nd, 1983, and the weeks that followed. Our genuine respect goes to the federal, state, and county law enforcement agencies of Omaha for their quick take-charge attitude in an emergency situation which was always professional, competent, and caring. We never lost confidence in any of them. Our most sincere gratitude to our neighbors, friends, military associates, teachers, Chris's classmates, restaurant owners, and volunteers who supported us during that trying time. Our thanks, too, to all those concerned citizens who heard about our situation by television or the newspapers, whose words of encouragement made a real difference. Some of you became friends, some of you we regret never meeting. With this kind of dedication, kindness, concern, and caring, it re-

stores your faith in mankind. Especially when you need it the most.

Thank you.

AFTERWORD

"Sure he's (Joubert) likeable, unless you're twelve years old and on your way to school. He's the most dangerous defendant I've ever dealt with."

Eric Wright
Maine Prosecutor

Thursday, October 4, 1990

I must confess I didn't do justice to Maine in my earlier description. Both times I was here before, winter's frozen grasp hid the beauty below. This time I arrived at autumn's peak. The colors of the changing leaves got more bright as detective Paul Kelley and I headed for the small town of Wiscasset, forty miles north of Portland. The trial had been moved there because of all the pretrial publicity. My attorney, Walt Diercks, had fought the subpeona and was trying to keep me from testifying in the case, but to no avail. The state's laws are very strict when it comes to reporters and the sources of their information. There was no shield to hide behind. John Joubert now stood trial for the murder of twelve-year-old Ricky Stetson, and the prosecution felt this book carried his confession at the top of Chapter Ten:

"I can't lie to you, I can't say I didn't do it, but the last time I plead guilty to anything I got the death penalty."

There was, of course, the circumstantial evidence: the bite mark, witnesses who saw the boy on the bicycle but nothing more. I had asked Joubert the question point blank on my last visit with him on Nebraska's Death Row. "Did you kill Ricky Stetson?"

Without much of a pause he extended his hand. Fumbling to find the right button he turned off my tape recorder. We sat quietly as Joubert struggled for words. Finally, he answered in an almost apologetic but frustrated manner. It was as if he wanted to tell me straight out, to get it off his conscience but couldn't. I took his answer as a yes, that he had killed the boy, and he wanted me to know the truth. I truly felt we had come too far for Joubert to lie.

Honestly, I cannot say whether I called the authorities in Maine to relay what I had been told. Sure, I felt an obligation to justice, but I also felt a strange allegiance to Joubert, the kind of feeling you get when you're told something you never really wanted to know. Now it seemed the biggest part of the case in Maine rested on my book and the now infamous quote at the top of Chapter Ten.

The forty-one-year-old Kelley, Irish of course and prematurely gray, had worked on the Stetson murder case from the day it happened. He had traveled to Nebraska to bring Joubert home to face the crime in what has turned out to be a precedent-setting case. The governors of the two states signed an agreement allowing Joubert to be tried for the murder but stating that he must return to face his death sentence in Nebraska as soon as the verdict was handed down. Kelley's job now was to ensure that I made it to court to testify. The prosecutors only wanted me to verify the quote in question. I was promised they would not come after my tapes or notes, a journalist's worst nightmare.

On the way to the courthouse we passed through the ship building town of Bath. The rough waters of the Kennebec River rubbed against two destroyers being refurbished for possible battle. The countryside was dotted with elegant old farmhouses and barns, seemingly untouched by time and trouble. The people of Wiscasset aren't even privy to Touch-tone phone service, but they would soon be privy to the bizzare workings of John Joubert's mind and fantasies.

Surprisingly, there were no reporters waiting for us as Kelley and I entered the courthouse.

"They're about to miss the biggest story of the day," the veteran investigator joked, and as it turned out he was right, and they did.

Just after three o'clock, I was called into the courtroom. For a solid hour I sat in the witness chair, for the first twenty minutes as the prosecution tried to paint me as an expert on the Joubert case, trying to convince the judge to allow my testimony. For the following forty minutes I was grilled by Joubert's court-appointed attorney Orrin Brown, a lumbering man. His gray suit hung uneasily on his frame, his face almost as red as his tie. From the start he was combative, pecking at me like a duck on a June bug. Repeatedly he tried to confuse me with his questions.

"You were brokering information to the police!" he barked.

"Objection!" called the assistant prosecutor Lisa Marchese, a petite blonde woman who had worked the deal to bring me to testify. "Asked and answered your honor. This is again becoming argumentative."

"Sustained," responded the judge, never looking up from the legal pad on which he was scribbling notes.

"I believe he said he wasn't working for the police, Mr. Brown."

Joubert's attorneys did their best to discredit me, but the judge decided the next morning my testimony was important and would be allowed. Again I felt caught somewhere between justice and Joubert.

Monday Oct. 15th.

After what had happened the first day, I was ready for the worst from Joubert's attorneys, expecting Orrin Brown to attack me with all his legal might. But to most everyone's surprise, he didn't do the questioning, leaving it to his assistant. I found her unprepared. It was basically my word against Joubert's, and she didn't even bother to ask if I had written down the quote in question or how I could remember it if I hadn't. The question never came, and John Joubert never had a chance.

The prosecution followed my testimony with that of bite experts and witnesses who had supposedly seen Joubert the night of the murder. Ten days later it was over. On October 15th, after only two hours of deliberations, John Joubert was found guilty of the murder of twelve-year-old Ricky Stetson. Prosecutors now hope he will get life in prison without parole, that is, if Nebraska doesn't carry out its "legal need to kill" first.

The last time I saw him, Joubert was being led away by security officers. He squinted his eyes to protect them from the bright fall sunshine. I had hoped to at least speak to him, but the time just never seemed right. As I walked down the courthouse steps to the car waiting for me, I stopped to speak with attorney Orrin Brown.

"Mr. Brown, when all this is over I'd like to talk with John again."

His answer was curt and to the point. "You can talk

with him after Nebraska executes him,'' he said, slamming the lid on the trunk of his car.

I didn't know quite what to say, so I didn't even try. I turned and walked away, taking one last look at the old courthouse and closing the book on what may very well be the biggest story of my career.